UK Complete
Air Fryer Cookbook

1777 Days Air Fryer Recipes Let you impress your friends and family with your culinary prowess!

Maria T. Hunt

CONTENTS

Introduction to Air Fryers

In recent years, the kitchen appliance market has witnessed the rise of a revolutionary cooking device - the Air Fryer. This innovative appliance has gained immense popularity for its ability to cook delicious and crispy meals with significantly less oil than traditional frying methods. In this comprehensive guide, we will delve into the advantages of using an Air Fryer, explore various tips and techniques for maximizing its potential, and provide insights into maintaining and cleaning this kitchen companion.

Advantages of Air Fryers

Healthier Cooking: One of the primary advantages of Air Fryers is their ability to cook food with minimal oil. Traditional frying methods can lead to excessive oil absorption, contributing to unhealthy diets. With Air Fryers, hot air circulates rapidly around the food, creating a crispy layer without submerging it in oil. This results in meals that are not only delicious but also healthier.

Time Efficiency: Air Fryers are known for their quick cooking times. The circulating hot air cooks food faster than conventional ovens, reducing overall cooking time. This is particularly beneficial for individuals with busy lifestyles who seek a convenient and efficient cooking solution.

Versatility: Air Fryers are incredibly versatile appliances that can handle a wide range of foods. From crispy french fries to juicy chicken wings, the Air Fryer can prepare a variety of dishes. Some models even come with additional features such as baking, grilling, and roasting capabilities, making them a multifunctional addition to any kitchen.

Energy Efficiency: Compared to traditional ovens, Air Fryers are more energy-efficient. Their compact size and quick cooking times contribute to lower energy consumption, making them an eco-friendly option for those conscious of their environmental impact.

Easy to Use: Air Fryers are designed with user-friendliness in mind. Most models come equipped with intuitive controls and preset cooking programs, making them accessible to both experienced cooks and beginners. The simplicity of operation adds to the overall appeal of Air Fryers.

Air Fryer Usage Tips and Techniques

Preheating: Preheating the Air Fryer is a crucial step for achieving optimal results. Just like traditional ovens, preheating ensures that the appliance reaches the desired temperature before placing the food inside, leading to more consistent and efficient cooking.

Proper Food Arrangement: To ensure even cooking, arrange food in a single layer, leaving space between each piece. This allows the hot air to circulate freely, preventing unevenly cooked or soggy results.

Oil Application: While Air Fryers significantly reduce the amount of oil needed for cooking, lightly coating the food with oil can enhance crispiness. Consider using a cooking spray or brushing a small amount of oil onto the food before air frying.

Shaking and Flipping: To achieve uniform crispiness, periodically shake or flip the food during the cooking process. This helps expose different parts of the food to the circulating hot air, preventing uneven browning.

Experiment with Temperatures and Times: Each Air Fryer model may have variations in temperature and cooking times. Experiment with different settings to find the perfect combination for your favorite recipes.

Air Fryer Cleaning and Maintenance

Regular Cleaning: To maintain optimal performance, it's essential to clean the Air Fryer regularly. Remove and clean the basket, tray, and other removable parts after each use. Refer to the manufacturer's instructions for specific cleaning guidelines.

Dealing with Residue: Stubborn food residue can be removed by soaking the removable parts in warm, soapy water. Use a soft brush or sponge to gently scrub away any remaining particles. Avoid abrasive materials that may damage the non-stick coating.

Cleaning the Interior: Wipe the interior of the Air Fryer with a damp cloth to remove any splatters or spills. Make sure the appliance is unplugged and has cooled down before cleaning the interior components.

Regular Inspection: Periodically inspect the power cord, plug, and other electrical components for any signs of damage. If you notice any issues, contact the manufacturer or a qualified technician for repairs.

Storage: When not in use, store the Air Fryer in a cool, dry place. Ensure proper ventilation to prevent the accumulation of moisture, which can lead to mold or unpleasant odors.

In conclusion, the Air Fryer has emerged as a game-changer in the culinary world, offering a healthier and more efficient way to enjoy crispy and delicious meals. By understanding its advantages, mastering usage tips and techniques, and adhering to proper cleaning and maintenance practices, you can make the most of this versatile kitchen appliance. Whether you are a seasoned chef or a kitchen novice, the Air Fryer is sure to become a staple in your culinary arsenal, bringing convenience and flavor to your everyday cooking adventures.

Breakfast & Snacks And Fries Recipes

Breakfast "pop Tarts"

Servings: 6

Ingredients:

- 2 slices of prepared pie crust, shortbread or filo will work fine
- 2 tbsp strawberry jam
- 60ml plain yogurt
- 1 tsp cornstarch
- 1 tsp Stevia sweetener
- 2 tbsp cream cheese
- A drizzle of olive oil

Directions:

1. Lay your pie crust flat and cut into 6 separate rectangular pieces
2. In a small bowl, mix together the cornstarch and the jam
3. Spread 1 tablespoon of the mixture on top of the crust
4. Fold each crust over to form the tart
5. Seal down the edges using a fork
6. Arrange your tarts inside the frying basket and spray with a little olive oil
7. Heat to 175ºC and cook for 10 minutes
8. Meanwhile, combine the yogurt, cream cheese and Stevia in a bowl
9. Remove the tarts and allow to cool
10. Once cool, add the frosting on top and sprinkle with the sugar sprinkles

Delicious Breakfast Casserole

Servings: 4

Ingredients:

- 4 frozen hash browns
- 8 sausages, cut into pieces
- 4 eggs
- 1 diced yellow pepper
- 1 diced green pepper
- 1 diced red pepper
- Half a diced onion

Directions:

1. Line the bottom of your fryer with aluminium foil and arrange the hash browns inside
2. Add the sausage on top (uncooked)
3. Now add the onions and the peppers, sprinkling evenly
4. Cook the casserole on 170ºC for around 10 minutes
5. Open your fryer and give the mixture a good stir
6. Combine the eggs in a small bowl and pour over the casserole, closing the lid
7. Cook for another 10 minutes on the same temperature
8. Serve with a little seasoning to taste

Raspberry Breakfast Pockets

Servings: 1

Ingredients:

- 2 slices of sandwich bread
- 1 tbsp soft cream cheese
- 1 tbsp raspberry jam
- 1 tbsp milk
- 1 egg

Directions:

1. Take one slice of the bread and add one tablespoon of jam into the middle
2. Take the second slice and add the cream cheese into the middle
3. Using a blunt knife, spread the jam and the cheese across the bread, but don't go to the outer edges
4. Take a small bowl and whisk the eggs and the milk together
5. Set your fryer to 190ºC and spray with a little oil
6. Dip your sandwich into the egg and arrange inside your fryer
7. Cook for 5 minutes on the first side, turn and cook for another 2 minutes

Loaded Hash Browns

Servings: 4

Ingredients:

- 4 large potatoes
- 2 tbsp bicarbonate of soda
- 1 tbsp salt
- 1 tbsp black pepper
- 1 tsp cayenne pepper
- 2 tbsp olive oil
- 1 large chopped onion
- 1 chopped red pepper
- 1 chopped green pepper

Directions:

1. Grate the potatoes
2. Squeeze out any water contained within the potatoes
3. Take a large bowl of water and add the potatoes
4. Add the bicarbonate of soda, combine everything and leave to soak for 25 minutes
5. Drain the water away and carefully pat the potatoes to dry
6. Transfer your potatoes into another bowl
7. Add the spices and oil
8. Combining everything well, tossing to coat evenly
9. Place your potatoes into your fryer basket
10. Set to 200ºC and cook for 10 minutes
11. Give the potatoes a shake and add the peppers and the onions
12. Cook for another 10 minutes

Hard Boiled Eggs Air Fryer Style

Servings: 2

Ingredients:

- 4 large eggs
- 1 tsp cayenne pepper
- Salt and pepper for seasoning

Directions:

1. Preheat the air fryer to 220°C
2. Take a wire rack and place inside the air fryer
3. Lay the eggs on the rack
4. Cook for between 15-17 minutes, depending upon how you like your eggs
5. Remove from the fryer and place in a bowl of cold water for around 5 minutes
6. Peel and season with the cayenne and the salt and pepper

Breakfast Sausage Burgers

Servings: 2

Ingredients:

- 8 links of your favourite sausage
- Salt and pepper to taste

Directions:

1. Remove the sausage from the skins and use a fork to create a smooth mixture
2. Season to your liking
3. Shape the sausage mixture into burgers or patties
4. Preheat your air fryer to 260°C
5. Arrange the burgers in the fryer, so they are not touching each other
6. Cook for 8 minutes
7. Serve still warm

Easy Cheese & Bacon Toasties

Servings: 2

Ingredients:

- 4 slices of sandwich bread
- 2 slices of cheddar cheese
- 5 slices of pre-cooked bacon
- 1 tbsp melted butter
- 2 slices of mozzarella cheese

Directions:

1. Take the bread and spread the butter onto one side of each slice
2. Place one slice of bread into the fryer basket, buttered side facing downwards
3. Place the cheddar on top, followed by the bacon, mozzarella and the other slice of bread on top, buttered side upwards
4. Set your fryer to 170ºC
5. Cook for 4 minutes and then turn over and cook for another 3 minutes
6. Serve whilst still hot

Oozing Baked Eggs

Servings: 2

Ingredients:

- 4 eggs
- 140g smoked gouda cheese, cut into small pieces
- Salt and pepper to taste

Directions:

1. You will need two ramekin dishes and spray each one before using
2. Crack two eggs into each ramekin dish
3. Add half of the Gouda cheese to each dish
4. Season and place into the air fryer
5. Cook at 350ºC for 15 minutes, until the eggs are cooked as you like them

Egg & Bacon Breakfast Cups

Servings: 8

Ingredients:

- 6 eggs
- 1 chopped red pepper
- 1 chopped green pepper
- 1 chopped yellow pepper
- 2 tbsp double cream
- 50g chopped spinach
- 50g grated cheddar cheese
- 50g grated mozzarella cheese
- 3 slices of cooked bacon, crumbled into pieces

Directions:

1. Take a large mixing bowl and crack the eggs
2. Add the cream and season with a little salt and pepper, combining everything well
3. Add the peppers, spinach, onions, both cheeses, and the crumbled bacon, combining everything once more
4. You will need silicone moulds or cups for this part, and you should pour equal amounts of the mixture into 8 cups
5. Cook at 150ºC for around 12 or 15 minutes, until the eggs are cooked properly

Healthy Stuffed Peppers

Servings: 2

Ingredients:

- 1 large bell pepper, deseeded and cut into halves
- 1 tsp olive oil
- 4 large eggs
- Salt and pepper to taste

Directions:

1. Take your peppers and rub a little olive oil on the edges
2. Into each pepper, crack one egg and season with salt and pepper
3. You will need to insert a trivet into your air fryer to hold the peppers, and then arrange the peppers evenly
4. Set your fryer to 200ºC and cook for 13 minutes
5. Once cooked, remove and serve with a little more seasoning, if required

Easy Omelette

Servings: 1

Ingredients:

- 50ml milk
- 2 eggs
- 60g grated cheese, any you like
- Any garnishes you like, such as mushrooms, peppers, etc.

Directions:

1. Take a small mixing bowl and crack the eggs inside, whisking with the milk
2. Add the salt and garnishes and combine again
3. Grease a 6x3" pan and pour the mixture inside
4. Arrange the pan inside the air fryer basket
5. Cook at 170ºC for 10 minutes
6. At the halfway point, sprinkle the cheese on top
7. Loosen the edges with a spatula before serving

Breakfast Doughnuts

Servings: 4

Ingredients:

- 1 packet of Pillsbury Grands
- 5 tbsp raspberry jam
- 1 tbsp melted butter
- 5 tbsp sugar

Directions:

1. Preheat your air fryer to 250ºC
2. Place the Pillsbury Grands into the air fryer and cook for around 5m minutes
3. Remove and place to one side
4. Take a large bowl and add the sugar
5. Coat the doughnuts in the melted butter, coating evenly
6. Dip into the sugar and coat evenly once more
7. Using an icing bag, add the jam into the bag and pipe an even amount into each doughnut
8. Eat warm or cold

Breakfast Eggs & Spinach

Servings: 4

Ingredients:

- 500g wilted, fresh spinach
- 200g sliced deli ham
- 1 tbsp olive oil
- 4 eggs
- 4 tsp milk
- Salt and pepper to taste
- 1 tbsp butter for cooking

Directions:

1. Preheat your air fryer to 180°C
2. You will need 4 small ramekin dishes, coated with a little butter
3. Arrange the wilted spinach, ham, 1 teaspoon of milk and 1 egg into each ramekin and season with a little salt and pepper
4. Place in the fryer 15 to 20 minutes, until the egg is cooked to your liking
5. Allow to cool before serving

Healthy Breakfast Bagels

Servings: 2

Ingredients:

- 170g self raising flour
- 120ml plain yogurt
- 1 egg

Directions:

1. Take a large mixing bowl, combine the flour and the yogurt to create a dough
2. Cover a flat surface with a little extra flour and set the dough down
3. Create four separate and even balls
4. Roll each ball out into a rope shape and form a bagel with each
5. Take a small mixing bowl and whisk the egg
6. Brush the egg over the top of the bagel
7. Arrange the bagels inside your fryer evenly
8. Cook at 170°C for 10 minutes
9. Allow to cool before serving

Morning Sausage Wraps

Servings: 8

Ingredients:

- 8 sausages, chopped into pieces
- 2 slices of cheddar cheese, cut into quarters
- 1 can of regular crescent roll dough
- 8 wooden skewers

Directions:

1. Take the dough and separate each one
2. Cut open the sausages evenly
3. The one of your crescent rolls and on the widest part, add a little sausage and then a little cheese
4. Roll the dough and tuck it until you form a triangle
5. Repeat this for four times and add into your air fryer
6. Cook at 190°C for 3 minutes
7. Remove your dough and add a skewer for serving
8. Repeat with the other four pieces of dough

Blanket Breakfast Eggs

Servings: 2

Ingredients:

- 2 eggs
- 2 slices of sandwich bread
- Olive oil spray
- Salt and pepper to taste

Directions:

1. Preheat your air fryer to 190°C and spray with a little oil
2. Meanwhile, take your bread and cut a hole into the middle of each piece
3. Place one slice inside your fryer and crack one egg into the middle
4. Season with a little salt and pepper
5. Cook for 5 minutes, before turning over and cooking for a further 2 minutes
6. Remove the first slice and repeat the process with the remaining slice of bread and egg

Mexican Breakfast Burritos

Servings: 6

Ingredients:

- 6 scrambled eggs
- 6 medium tortillas
- Half a minced red pepper
- 8 sausages, cut into cubes and browned
- 4 pieces of bacon, pre-cooked and cut into pieces
- 65g grated cheese of your choice
- A small amount of olive oil for cooking

Directions:

1. Into a regular mixing bowl, combine the eggs, bell pepper, bacon pieces, the cheese, and the browned sausage, giving everything a good stir
2. Take your first tortilla and place half a cup of the mixture into the middle, folding up the top and bottom and rolling closed
3. Repeat until all your tortillas have been used
4. Arrange the burritos into the bottom of your fryer and spray with a little oil
5. Cook the burritos at 170ºC for 5 minutes

Cheesy Sausage Breakfast Pockets

Servings: 2

Ingredients:

- 1 packet of regular puff pastry
- 4 sausages, cooked and crumbled into pieces
- 5 eggs
- 50g cooked bacon
- 50g grated cheddar cheese

Directions:

1. Scramble your eggs in your usual way
2. Add the sausage and the bacon as you are cooking the eggs and combine well
3. Take your pastry sheets and cut rectangular shapes
4. Add a little of the egg and meat mixture to one half of each pastry piece
5. Fold the rectangles over and use a fork to seal down the edges
6. Place your pockets into your air fryer and cook at 190ºC for 10 minutes
7. Allow to cool before serving

Your Favourite Breakfast Bacon

Servings: 2

Ingredients:

- 4-5 rashers of lean bacon, fat cut off
- Salt and pepper for seasoning

Directions:

1. Line your air fryer basket with parchment paper
2. Place the bacon in the basket
3. Set the fryer to 200°C
4. Cook for 10 minutes for crispy. If you want it very crispy, cook for another 2 minutes

Tangy Breakfast Hash

Servings: 6

Ingredients:

- 2 tbsp olive oil
- 2 sweet potatoes, cut into cubes
- 1 tbsp smoked paprika
- 1 tsp salt
- 1 tsp black pepper
- 2 slices of bacon, cut into small pieces

Directions:

1. Preheat your air fryer to 200°C
2. Pour the olive oil into a large mixing bowl
3. Add the bacon, seasonings, potatoes and toss to evenly coat
4. Transfer the mixture into the air fryer and cook for 12-16 minutes
5. Stir after 10 minutes and continue to stir periodically for another 5 minutes

Apple Crisps

Servings: 2

Ingredients:

- 2 apples, chopped
- 1 tsp cinnamon
- 2 tbsp brown sugar
- 1 tsp lemon juice
- 2.5 tbsp plain flour
- 3 tbsp oats
- 2 tbsp cold butter
- Pinch of salt

Directions:

1. Preheat the air fryer to 260ºC
2. Take a 5" baking dish and crease
3. Take a large bowl and combine the apples with the sugar, cinnamon and lemon juice
4. Add the mixture to the baking dish and cover with aluminium foil
5. Place in the air fryer and cook for 15 minutes
6. Open the lid and cook for another 5 minutes
7. Combine the rest of the ingredients in a food processor, until a crumble-type mixture occurs
8. Add over the top of the cooked apples
9. Cook with the lid open for another 5 minutes
10. Allow to cool a little before serving

French Toast

Servings: 2

Ingredients:

- 2 beaten eggs
- 2 tbsp softened butter
- 4 slices of sandwich bread
- 1 tsp cinnamon
- 1 tsp nutmeg
- 1 tsp ground cloves
- 1 tsp maple syrup

Directions:

1. Preheat your fryer to 180ºC
2. Take a bowl and add the eggs, salt, cinnamon, nutmeg, and cloves, combining well
3. Take your bread and butter each side, cutting into strips
4. Dip the bread slices into the egg mixture
5. Arrange each slice into the basket of your fryer
6. Cook for 2 minutes
7. Take the basket out and spray with a little cooking spray
8. Turn over the slices and place back into the fryer
9. Cook for 4 minutes
10. Remove and serve with maple syrup

Sauces & Snack And Appetiser Recipes

Salt And Vinegar Chickpeas

Servings: 5

Ingredients:

- 1 can chickpeas
- 100ml white vinegar
- 1 tbsp olive oil
- Salt to taste

Directions:

1. Combine chickpeas and vinegar in a pan, simmer remove from heat and stand for 30 minutes
2. Preheat the air fryer to 190°C
3. Drain chickpeas
4. Place chickpeas in the air fryer and cook for about 4 minutes
5. Pour chickpeas into an ovenproof bowl drizzle with oil, sprinkle with salt
6. Place bowl in the air fryer and cook for another 4 minutes

Spicy Peanuts

Servings: 8

Ingredients:

- 2 tbsp olive oil
- 3 tbsp seafood seasoning
- ½ tsp cayenne
- 300g raw peanuts
- Salt to taste

Directions:

1. Preheat the air fryer to 160°C
2. Whisk together ingredients in a bowl and stir in the peanuts
3. Add to air fryer and cook for 10 minutes, shake then cook for a further 10 minutes
4. Sprinkle with salt and cook for another 5 minutes

Tasty Pumpkin Seeds

Servings: 2

Ingredients:

- 1 ¾ cups pumpkin seeds
- 2 tsp avocado oil
- 1 tsp paprika
- 1 tsp salt

Directions:

1. Preheat air fryer to 180ºC
2. Add all ingredients to a bowl and mix well
3. Place in the air fryer and cook for 35 minutes shaking frequently

Tostones

Servings: 4

Ingredients:

- 2 unripe plantains
- Olive oil cooking spray
- 300ml of water
- Salt to taste

Directions:

1. Preheat the air fryer to 200ºC
2. Slice the tips off the plantain
3. Cut the plantain into 1 inch chunks
4. Place in the air fryer spray with oil and cook for 5 minutes
5. Remove the plantain from the air fryer and smash to ½ inch pieces
6. Soak in a bowl of salted water
7. Remove from the water and return to the air fryer season with salt cook for 5 minutes
8. Turn and cook for another 5 minutes

Air Fryer Mozzarella-stuffed Meatballs

Servings: 4
Cooking Time: 10 Mints
Ingredients:

- 450 g beef mince
- 50 g bread crumbs
- 25 g freshly grated Parmesan
- 5 g freshly chopped parsley
- 1 large egg
- 2 cloves garlic, crushed
- 1 tsp. dried oregano
- Salt
- Freshlyground black pepper
- 85 g fresh mozzarella, cut into 16 cubes
- Marinara, for serving

Directions:

1. In a large bowl, combine beef, bread crumbs, Parmesan, parsley, egg, garlic, and oregano. Season with salt and pepper.
2. Scoop about 2 tablespoons of meat and flatten into a patty in your hand. Place a cube of mozzarella in the centre and pinch meat up around cheese and roll into a ball. Repeat with remaining meat to make 16 total meatballs.
3. Working in batches as needed, place meatballs in basket of air fryer and cook at 190°C/375°F for 12 minutes.
4. Serve with warmed marinara

Air Fryer Chili Cheese Dogs

Servings: 4
Cooking Time: 10 Mints
Ingredients:

- 4 hot dog buns
- 4 hot dogs
- 240 ml chili
- 57 g shredded cheddar cheese
- oil for spraying

Directions:

1. Add a light spray or brush of oil on the hot dogs. Place the hot dogs in the air fryer basket.
2. Air Fry at 380°F/193°C for 8-10 minutes depending on your preferred texture and size of hot dogs. If you like your hot dogs extra crispy, air fry at 400°F/200°C for about 6-8 minutes. Flip the hot dogs half way through cooking.
3. Heat the chili while the hot dogs cook. Set aside.
4. Place hot dogs in buns then add chili and cheese on top. Cook in the air fryer for about one minute to warm and crisp the bread, cheese and chili.

Muhammara

Servings: 4

Ingredients:

- 4 romano peppers
- 4 tablespoons olive oil
- 100 g/1 cup walnuts
- 90 g/1 heaped cup dried breadcrumbs
- 1 teaspoon cumin
- 2 tablespoons pomegranate molasses
- freshly squeezed juice of ½ a lemon
- ½ teaspoon chilli/chili salt (or salt and some chilli/hot red pepper flakes combined)
- fresh pomegranate seeds, to serve

Directions:

1. Preheat the air-fryer to 180ºC/350ºF.
2. Rub the peppers with ½ teaspoon of the olive oil. Add the peppers to the preheated air-fryer and air-fry for 8 minutes.
3. Meanwhile, lightly toast the walnuts by tossing them in a shallow pan over a medium heat for 3–5 minutes. Allow to cool, then grind the walnuts in a food processor. Once the peppers are cooked, chop off the tops and discard most of the seeds. Add to the food processor with all other ingredients. Process until smooth. Allow to cool in the fridge, then serve the dip with pomegranate seeds on top.

Air Fryer Canned Crescent Rolls

Servings: 2

Cooking Time: 9 Mints

Ingredients:

- 1 can refrigerated Crescent Rolls
- oil spray

Directions:

1. Spray the air fryer basket or racks with oil to keep the crescent rolls from sticking.
2. Lay crescent rolls in a single layer on an air fryer basket/rack. Make sure to space them out so they aren't touching & have room to rise & expand.
3. Air Fry at 330°F/165°C for about 6-7 minutes. Gently wiggle to loosen from the baskets.
4. If needed, continue to Air Fry for another 1-3 minutes, or until they are crispy brown and cooked through.

Air-fried Pickles

Servings: 4

Ingredients:

- 1/2 cup mayonnaise
- 2 tsp sriracha sauce
- 1 jar dill pickle slices
- 1 egg
- 2 tbsp milk
- 50g flour
- 50g cornmeal
- ½ tsp seasoned salt
- ¼ tsp paprika
- ¼ tsp garlic powder
- ⅛ tsp pepper
- Cooking spray

Directions:

1. Mix the mayo and sriracha together in a bowl and set aside
2. Heat the air fryer to 200ºC
3. Drain the pickles and pat dry
4. Mix egg and milk together, in another bowl mix all the remaining ingredients
5. Dip the pickles in the egg mix then in the flour mix
6. Spray the air fryer with cooking spray
7. Cook for about 4 minutes until crispy

Jalapeño Pockets

Servings: 4

Ingredients:

- 1 chopped onion
- 60g cream cheese
- 1 jalapeño, chopped
- 8 wonton wrappers
- ¼ tsp garlic powder
- ⅛ tsp onion powder

Directions:

1. Cook the onion in a pan for 5 minutes until softened
2. Add to a bowl and mix with the remaining ingredients
3. Lay the wonton wrappers out and add filling to each one
4. Fold over to create a triangle and seal with water around the edges
5. Heat the air fryer to 200ºC
6. Place in the air fryer and cook for about 4 minutes

Onion Bahji

Servings: 8

Ingredients:

- 1 sliced red onion
- 1 sliced onion
- 1 tsp salt
- 1 minced jalapeño pepper
- 150g chickpea flour
- 4 tbsp water
- 1 clove garlic, minced
- 1 tsp coriander
- 1 tsp chilli powder
- 1 tsp turmeric
- ½ tsp cumin

Directions:

1. Place all ingredients in a bowl and mix well, leave to rest for 10 minutes
2. Preheat air fryer to 175ºC
3. Spray air fryer with cooking spray.
4. Form mix into bahji shapes and add to air fryer
5. Cook for 6 minutes turn and cook for a further 6 minutes

Potato Fries

Servings: 2

Ingredients:

- 2 large potatoes (baking potato size)
- 1 teaspoon olive oil
- salt

Directions:

1. Peel the potatoes and slice into fries about 5 x 1.5cm/¾ x ¾ in. by the length of the potato. Submerge the fries in a bowl of cold water and place in the fridge for about 10 minutes.
2. Meanwhile, preheat the air-fryer to 160ºC/325ºF.
3. Drain the fries thoroughly, then toss in the oil and season. Tip into the preheated air-fryer in a single layer (you may need to cook them in two batches, depending on the size of your air-fryer). Air-fry for 15 minutes, tossing once during cooking by shaking the air-fryer drawer, then increase the temperature of the air-fryer to 200ºC/400ºF and cook for a further 3 minutes. Serve immediately.

Air Fryer White Castle Frozen Sliders

Servings: 3
Cooking Time: 6 Mints
Ingredients:

- 6 frozen White Castle Sliders
- OPTIONAL CONDIMENTS:
- Ketchup, mustard, bbq sauce, pickles , etc

Directions:

1. Do not preheat the air fryer. Using a fork, carefully remove the top bun to expose the meat. Set top bun aside.
2. Place just the bottom bun and patty in the air fryer, meat side up.
3. Air Fry the just the bottom bun with meat and cheese at 340°F/171°C for 5 minutes.
4. Add the top bun to the air fryer next to bottom buns (not on top of). Air fry for 1 minute until top bun is warmed. If you want the slider hotter and crisper, air fry for another 1-2 minutes.
5. Add ketchup, mustard or whatever else you love on your sliders, top with the bun and enjoy!

Tortellini Bites

Servings: 6
Ingredients:

- 200g cheese tortellini
- 150g flour
- 100g panko bread crumbs
- 50g grated parmesan
- 1 tsp dried oregano
- 2 eggs
- ½ tsp garlic powder
- ½ tsp chilli flakes
- Salt
- Pepper

Directions:

1. Cook the tortellini according to the packet instructions
2. Mix the panko, parmesan, oregano, garlic powder, chilli flakes salt and pepper in a bowl
3. Beat the eggs in another bowl and place the flour in a third bowl
4. Coat the tortellini in flour, then egg and then in the panko mix
5. Place in the air fryer and cook at 185ºC for 10 minutes until crispy
6. Serve with marinara sauce for dipping

Sweet Potato Fries

Servings: 4

Ingredients:

- 2 medium sweet potatoes
- 2 teaspoons olive oil
- ½ teaspoon salt
- ½ teaspoon chilli/hot red pepper flakes
- ½ teaspoon smoked paprika

Directions:

1. Preheat the air-fryer to 190ºC/375ºF.
2. Peel the sweet potatoes and slice into fries about 1 x 1 cm/½ x ½ in. by the length of the potato. Toss the sweet potato fries in the oil, salt, chilli and paprika, making sure every fry is coated.
3. Tip into the preheated air-fryer in a single layer (you may need to cook them in two batches, depending on the size of your air-fryer). Air-fry for 10 minutes, turning once halfway during cooking. Serve immediately.

Air Fryer Salt And Vinegar Potato Gems

Servings: 5-6

Cooking Time: 40 Mints

Ingredients:

- 1kg washed desiree potatoes
- 1 tbsp malt vinegar, plus extra, to serve
- 22 g grated parmesan
- 2 tbsp plain flour
- 1/2 tsp sea salt, plus extra, to serve
- 1 tsp onion powder
- 1/2 tsp garlic powder
- Tomato sauce, to serve

Directions:

1. Cook the potatoes in boiling water for 10 minutes. Drain well and set aside until cool enough to handle. Peel, then grate into a bowl. Drizzle with vinegar and set aside, tossing occasionally, or until cool.
2. Combine the parmesan , flour , salt , onion powder and garlic powder . Toss through the potato. Shape 1 tbsp mixture into a tube. Place on a tray. Repeat with remaining mixture. Place in the fridge for 30 minutes.
3. Place half the gems in the basket of an airfryer and spray with oil. Air fry at 200°C/400°F for 15 minutes. Repeat with remaining gems.
4. Arrange gems on a serving plate and sprinkle with extra salt and vinegar. Serve with tomato sauce on the side

Pork Jerky

Servings: 35
Ingredients:

- 300g mince pork
- 1 tbsp oil
- 1 tbsp sriracha
- 1 tbsp soy
- ½ tsp pink curing salt
- 1 tbsp rice vinegar
- ½ tsp salt
- ½ tsp pepper
- ½ tsp onion powder

Directions:

1. Mix all ingredients in a bowl until combined
2. Refrigerate for about 8 hours
3. Shape into sticks and place in the air fryer
4. Heat the air fryer to 160ºC
5. Cook for 1 hour turn then cook for another hour
6. Turn again and cook for another hour
7. Cover with paper and sit for 8 hours

Air Fryer Garlic Bread

Servings: 4
Cooking Time: 30 Mints
Ingredients:

- Homemade garlic butter(2 tablespoons of butter
- 3 garlic cloves and 2 tablespoons of fresh parsley).
- A crusty baguette, day old roll or even just sliced bread all great for making garlic bread.

Directions:

1. slice your bread.
2. Then crush your garlic cloves with a crusher, or in a pestle and mortar.
3. Place the garlic into a microwaveable bowl, add the butter and parsley.
4. Microwave for 10 seconds bursts until the butter has melted.
5. Place into the air fryer basket.
6. Bake at 200°C/400°F for 6 minutes.

Beetroot Crisps

Servings: 2

Ingredients:

- 3 medium beetroots
- 2 tbsp oil
- Salt to taste

Directions:

1. Peel and thinly slice the beetroot
2. Coat with the oil and season with salt
3. Preheat the air fryer to 200ºC
4. Place in the air fryer and cook for 12-18 minutes until crispy

Avocado Fries

Servings: 2

Ingredients:

- 35 g/¼ cup plain/all-purpose flour (gluten free if you wish)
- ½ teaspoon chilli/chili powder
- 1 egg, beaten
- 50 g/heaped ½ cup dried breadcrumbs
- 1 avocado, skin and stone removed, and each half sliced lengthways
- salt and freshly ground black pepper

Directions:

1. Preheat the air-fryer to 200ºC/400ºF.
2. In a bowl combine the flour and chilli/chili powder, then season with salt and pepper. Place the beaten egg in a second bowl and the breadcrumbs in a third bowl.
3. Dip each avocado slice in the seasoned flour (shaking off any excess), then the egg and finally the breadcrumbs.
4. Add the breaded avocado slices to the preheated air-fryer and air-fry for 6 minutes, turning after 4 minutes. Serve immediately.

Cheese Wontons

Servings: 8

Ingredients:

- 8 wonton wrappers
- 1 carton pimento cheese
- Small dish of water
- Cooking spray

Directions:

1. Place one tsp of cheese in the middle of each wonton wrapper
2. Brush the edges of each wonton wrapper with water
3. Fold over to create a triangle and seal
4. Heat the air fryer to 190°C
5. Spray the wontons with cooking spray
6. Place in the air fryer and cook for 3 minutes
7. Turnover and cook for a further 3 minutes

Ultra Crispy Air Fryer Chickpeas

Servings: 2

Cooking Time: 15 Mints

Ingredients:

- 250 g can of chickpeas (drained and rinsed)
- 1 tablespoon olive oil
- ⅛ teaspoon salt
- ¼ teaspoon garlic powder
- ¼ teaspoon onion powder
- ½ teaspoon paprika

Directions:

1. Heat air fryer to 200°C/400° .
2. Drain and rinse chickpeas (no need to dry). Toss with olive oil and spices.
3. Dump the whole batch of chickpeas in the air fryer basket. Cook for 12-15 minutes, shaking a couple of times.
4. When chickpeas are cooked to your liking, remove from air fryer, taste and add more salt and pepper to taste.
5. Store in an open container.

Poultry Recipes
__Buffalo Chicken Wontons__

Servings: 6

Ingredients:

- 200g shredded chicken
- 1 tbsp buffalo sauce
- 4 tbsp softened cream cheese
- 1 sliced spring onion
- 2 tbsp blue cheese crumbles
- 12 wonton wrappers

Directions:

1. Preheat the air fryer to 200°C
2. Take a bowl and combine the chicken and buffalo sauce
3. In another bowl mix the cream cheese until a smooth consistency has formed and then combine the scallion blue cheese and seasoned chicken
4. Take the wonton wrappers and run wet fingers along each edge
5. Place 1 tbsp of the filling into the centre of the wonton and fold the corners together
6. Cook at 200°C for 3 to 5 minutes, until golden brown

__Spicy Chicken Wing Drummettes__

Servings: 4

Ingredients:

- 10 large chicken drumettes
- Cooking spray
- 100ml rice vinegar
- 3 tbsp honey
- 2 tbsp unsalted chicken stock
- 1 tbsp lower sodium soy sauce
- 1 tbsp toasted sesame oil
- ⅜ tsp crushed red pepper
- 1 garlic clove, finely chopped
- 2 tbsp chopped, unsalted, roasted peanuts
- 1 tbsp chopped fresh chives

Directions:

1. Coat the chicken in cooking spray and place inside the air fryer
2. Cook at 200°C for 30 minutes
3. Take a mixing bowl and combine the vinegar, honey, stock, soy sauce, oil, crushed red pepper and garlic
4. Cook to a simmer, until a syrup consistency is achieved
5. Coat the chicken in this mixture and sprinkle with peanuts and chives

Olive Stained Turkey Breast

Servings: 14

Ingredients:

- The brine from a can of olives
- 150ml buttermilk
- 300g boneless and skinless turkey breasts
- 1 sprig fresh rosemary
- 2 sprigs fresh thyme

Directions:

1. Take a mixing bowl and combine the olive brine and buttermilk
2. Pour the mixture over the turkey breast
3. Add the rosemary and thyme sprigs
4. Place into the refrigerator for 8 hours
5. Remove from the fridge and let the turkey reach room temperature
6. Preheat the air fryer to 175C
7. Cook for 15 minutes, ensuring the turkey is cooked through before serving

Chicken And Cheese Chimichangas

Servings: 6

Ingredients:

- 100g shredded chicken (cooked)
- 150g nacho cheese
- 1 chopped jalapeño pepper
- 6 flour tortillas
- 5 tbsp salsa
- 60g refried beans
- 1 tsp cumin
- 0.5 tsp chill powder
- Salt and pepper to taste

Directions:

1. Take a large mixing bowl and add all of the ingredients, combining well
2. Add ⅓ of the filling to each tortilla and roll into a burrito shape
3. Spray the air fryer with cooking spray and heat to 200ºC
4. Place the chimichangas in the air fryer and cook for 7 minutes

Keto Tandoori Chicken

Servings: 2

Ingredients:

- 500g chicken tenders, halved
- 1 tbsp minced ginger
- 1 tbsp minced garlic
- 1 tsp cayenne pepper
- 1 tsp turmeric
- 1 tsp garam masala
- 60ml yogurt
- 25g coriander leaves
- Salt and pepper to taste

Directions:

1. Take a large mixing bowl and combine all the ingredients, except the chicken
2. Once combined, add the chicken to the bowl and make sure it is fully coated
3. Preheat the air fryer to 160ºC
4. Place the chicken in the air fryer and baste with oil
5. Cook for 10 minutes, turning over and then cooking for another 5 minutes
6. Serve whilst still warm

Cheddar & Bbq Stuffed Chicken

Servings: 2

Ingredients:

- 3 strips of bacon
- 100g cheddar cheese
- 3 tbsp barbecue sauce
- 300g skinless and boneless chicken breasts
- salt and ground pepper to taste

Directions:

1. Preheat the air fryer to 190ºC
2. Cook one of the back strips for 2 minutes, before cutting into small pieces
3. Increase the temperature of the air fryer to 200ºC
4. Mix together the cooked bacon, cheddar cheese and 1 tbsp barbecue sauce
5. Take the chicken and make a pouch by cutting a 1 inch gap into the top
6. Stuff the pouch with the bacon and cheese mixture and then wrap around the chicken breast
7. Coat the chicken with the rest of the BBQ sauce
8. Cook for 10 minutes in the air fryer, before turning and cooking for an additional 10 minutes

Air Fryer Chicken Tenders

Servings: 4
Cooking Time: 15 Mints

Ingredients:

- 675 g chicken tenders
- Salt
- Freshly ground black pepper
- 195 g plain flour
- 250 g panko bread crumbs
- 2 large eggs
- 60 ml buttermilk
- Cooking spray
- FOR THE HONEY MUSTARD
- 3 tbsp. honey
- 2 tbsp. dijon mustard
- 1/4 tsp. hot sauce (optional)
- Pinch of salt
- 80 g mayonnaise
- Freshlyground black pepper

Directions:

1. Season chicken tenders on both sides with salt and pepper. Place flour and bread crumbs in two separate shallow bowls. In a third bowl, whisk together eggs and buttermilk. Working one at a time, dip chicken in flour, then egg mixture, and finally in bread crumbs, pressing to coat.

2. Working in batches, place chicken tenders in basket of air fryer, being sure to not overcrowd it. Spray the tops of chicken with cooking spray and cook at 200°C/400°F for 5 minutes. Flip chicken over, spray the tops with more cooking spray and cook 5 minutes more. Repeat with remaining chicken tenders.

3. Make sauce: In a small bowl, whisk together mayonnaise, honey, dijon, and hot sauce, if using. Season with a pinch of salt and a few cracks of black pepper.

4. Serve chicken tenders with honey mustard

Bacon Wrapped Chicken Thighs

Servings: 4

Ingredients:

- 75g softened butter
- ½ clove minced garlic
- ¼ tsp dried thyme
- ¼ tsp dried basil
- ⅛ tsp coarse salt
- 100g thick cut bacon
- 350g chicken thighs, boneless and skinless
- 2 tsp minced garlic
- Salt and pepper to taste

Directions:

1. Take a mixing bowl and add the softened butter, garlic, thyme, basil, salt and pepper, combining well
2. Place the butter onto a sheet of plastic wrap and roll up to make a butter log
3. Refrigerate for about 2 hours
4. Remove the plastic wrap
5. Place one bacon strip onto the butter and then place the chicken thighs on top of the bacon. Sprinkle with garlic
6. Place the cold butter into the middle of the chicken thigh and tuck one end of bacon into the chicken
7. Next, fold over the chicken thigh whilst rolling the bacon around
8. Repeat with the rest
9. Preheat the air fryer to 188C
10. Cook the chicken until white in the centre and the juices run clear

Air Fryer Peri Peri Chicken

Servings: 4

Cooking Time: 30 Mints

Ingredients:

- 640 g chicken mini fillets
- Peri peri seasoning

Directions:

1. Add the chicken mini fillets to a bowl.
2. Add the peri peri seasoning and then massage it all over the chicken breasts.
3. Place the chicken fillets into the air fryer basket.
4. Cook for 20 minutes at 200°C/400°F, turning the chicken when the cooking time is 10 minutes in.
5. When cooking, if you overcrowd your air fryer basket then ensure that you give it a good shake at least every 5 minutes while cooking.
6. Check the temperature of your peri peri chicken before serving, to ensure it is 74°C/165°F internally.

Air Fryer Chicken Drumsticks

Servings: 4
Cooking Time: 25 Mints
Ingredients:

- 8 - 12 chicken drumsticks
- Seasoning
- Oil (optional)

Directions:

1. Preheat the air fryer to 200°C/400°F for 5 minutes.
2. Optionally brush the drumsticks with some oil.
3. Season the chicken drumsticks with your favourite spices. You can just use salt if you prefer.
4. Add the drumsticks to the air fryer basket. You might need to use a trivet to fit them all in, or if you have a smaller air fryer, cook them in batches.
5. Cook for 22 - 25 minutes, turning halfway through.
6. Check the chicken is cooked all the way through - they should reach 75°C/165°F internally, use a meat thermometer if possible.

Air Fryer Chicken Strips

Servings: 4
Cooking Time: 15 Mints
Ingredients:

- 454 g chicken tenders , or boneless skinless chicken breast, tenders, or thighs
- 240-480 ml Panko – or breading of choice-breadcrumbs, crushed pork rinds, almond flour, etc
- 2 eggs
- 1 teaspoon salt , or to taste
- 1/2 teaspoon black pepper , or to taste
- 1 teaspoon garlic powder
- 1 teaspoon paprik

Directions:

1. Preheat the Air Fryer at 370°F/188°C for 4 minutes.
2. If not using tenders, cut the chicken into strips. Make sure they are evenly sized. The thicker they are, the longer they will take to cook.
3. Combine the seasonings (salt, pepper, garlic powder and paprika). Season the chicken strips with the spices. Put the Panko (or breading of choice) in a bowl large enough to dredge the chicken. In another bowl, beat the eggs until smooth.
4. Coat the chicken cutlets strips in egg, then in the Panko (or breading of choice). Press chicken strips into the Panko so that it sticks and completely coats the chicken. Repeat for all chicken pieces.
5. Generously spray both sides of all the coated chicken with oil spray to coat all dry spots.
6. Air Fry at 370°F/190°C for 6 minutes. Gently flip the tenders and lightly spray any dry spots. Continue to air fry for another 2-8 minutes (depending on the size and thickness of your tenders), or until they are crispy brown or internal temperature of the chicken reaches 165°F/74°C.

Air Fryer Chicken Fajitas Recipe

Servings: 4-6
Cooking Time: 20 Mints
Ingredients:

- 640 g chicken mini fillets
- 3 mixed peppers
- 2 white onions
- Fajita seasoning

Directions:
1. Slice your bell peppers and onions.
2. Add your chicken breasts to a bowl.
3. Spread the fajita seasoning over the top of the chicken and then rub it across the breasts well.
4. Add the chicken mini fillets to the basket.
5. Cook at 200°C/400°F for 10 minutes.
6. Add the onion and peppers.
7. Cook at 200°C/400°F for another 10 minutes.

Air Fryer Rotisserie Chicken

Servings: 6
Cooking Time: 20 Mints
Ingredients:

- 1.3kg chicken, cut into 8 pieces
- Salt
- Freshlyground black pepper
- 1 tbsp. dried thyme
- 2 tsp. dried oregano
- 2 tsp. garlic powder
- 2 tsp. onion powder
- 1 tsp. smoked paprika
- 1/4 tsp. cayenn

Directions:
1. Season chicken pieces all over with salt and pepper. In a medium bowl, whisk to combine herbs and spices, then rub spice mix all over chicken pieces.
2. Add dark meat pieces to air fryer basket and cook at 180°C/350°F for 10 minutes, then flip and cook 10 minutes more. Repeat with chicken breasts, but reduce time to 8 minutes per side. Use a meat thermometer to insure that chicken is cooked through, each piece should register 73°C/165°F.

Jerk Chicken

Servings: 8

Cooking Time: 45 Mints

Ingredients:

- 8 chicken leg quarters or chicken drumsticks
- 80 ml apple cider vinegar
- 80 ml dark soy sauce
- 60 ml lime juice
- 120 ml orange juice
- 1 tbsp. allspice
- 1 tsp. black pepper
- 1 tsp. cinnamon
- 2 tsp. fresh thyme
- 3 spring onions, chopped
- 2 tbsp. ginger, peeled and chopped
- 1 medium onion, chopped
- 8 garlic cloves, peeled
- 4 Scotch bonnets, seeds removed

Directions:

1. Pat the skin of your chicken dry and using a knife make small holes all around the chicken.

2. In a blender combine all remaining ingredients and blend for three minutes. Pour half the jerk marinade over the chicken and massage it in. Refrigerate overnight.

3. When ready to cook, bring grill temperature up to 165°C/330°F. Place the chicken skin side down and close BBQ lid for 5-7 minutes until it starts to brown. Turn over and cook for the remaining 5-7 minutes. Repeat twice more until chicken is dark brown and cooked all the way through.

4. Move chicken to the sides of the grill and brush remaining jerk sauce on top. Close the lid and cook for a further 5-7minutes.

5. Remove from BBQ and leave chicken to cool for around 10 minutes. Either eat on the bone or chop the meat into smaller pieces and serve.

Quick Chicken Nuggets

Servings: 4

Ingredients:

- 500g chicken tenders
- 25g ranch salad dressing mixture
- 2 tbsp plain flour
- 100g breadcrumbs
- 1 egg, beaten
- Olive oil spray

Directions:

1. Take a large mixing bowl and arrange the chicken inside
2. Sprinkle the seasoning over the top and ensure the chicken is evenly coated
3. Place the chicken to one side for around 10 minutes
4. Add the flour into a resealable bag
5. Crack the egg into a small mixing bowl and whisk
6. Pour the breadcrumbs onto a medium sized plate
7. Transfer the chicken into the resealable bag and coat with the flour, giving it a good shake
8. Remove the chicken and dip into the egg, and then rolling it into the breadcrumbs, coating evenly
9. Repeat with all pieces of the chicken
10. Heat your air fryer to 200ºC
11. Arrange the chicken inside the fryer and add a little olive oil spray to avoid sticking
12. Cook for 4 minutes, before turning over and cooking for another 4 minutes
13. Remove and serve whilst hot

Air Fryer Chicken Parmesan

Servings: 4
Cooking Time: 10 Mints

Ingredients:

- 2 large boneless chicken breasts
- Salt
- Freshlyground black pepper
- 40 g plain flour
- 2 large eggs
- 100 g panko bread crumbs
- 25 g freshly grated Parmesan
- 1 tsp. dried oregano
- 1/2 tsp.
- garlic powder
- 1/2 tsp. chilli flakes
- 240 g marinara/tomato sauce
- 100 g grated mozzarella
- Freshly chopped parsley, for garnish

Directions:

1. Pat the skin of your chicken dry and using a knife make small holes all around the chicken.

2. In a blender combine all remaining ingredients and blend for three minutes. Pour half the jerk marinade over the chicken and massage it in. Refrigerate overnight.

3. When ready to cook, bring grill temperature up to 165°C/330°F. Place the chicken skin side down and close BBQ lid for 5-7 minutes until it starts to brown. Turn over and cook for the remaining 5-7 minutes. Repeat twice more until chicken is dark brown and cooked all the way through.

4. Move chicken to the sides of the grill and brush remaining jerk sauce on top. Close the lid and cook for a further 5-7minutes.

5. Remove from BBQ and leave chicken to cool for around 10 minutes. Either eat on the bone or chop the meat into smaller pieces and serve.

Air Fryer Rosemary Chicken Breast

Servings: 2
Cooking Time: 20 Mints
Ingredients:

- 2 chicken breasts (1 per person)
- Spray oil
- Salt and pepper
- 1/4 teaspoon smoked paprika
- 1/4 teaspoon garlic salt or garlic powder
- 1 spray of rosemary

Directions:

1. Remove the rosemary leaves from the sprig and chop finely.
2. Add to a bowl with the salt, pepper, garlic powder and a few sprays of oil, or 1/4 teaspoon. Mix well.
3. Brush this mix onto both sides of your chicken breast.
4. Add to the air fryer basket. Cook at 180°C/360°F for 10 minutes.
5. Turn over and spray lightly with oil again if needed.Cook at 180°C/360°F for another 10 minutes.
6. Check that the internal temperature of the rosemary chicken breast is a minimum of 74°C/165°F and then remove from the air fryer.

Air Fryer Cajun Chicken Recipe

Servings: 5
Cooking Time: 30 Mints
Ingredients:

- 640 g chicken mini fillets
- Cajun seasoning

Directions:

1. Add chicken to a bowl.
2. Add cajun seasoning and rub all over the chicken fillets.
3. Add your chicken mini fillets to the air fryer.
4. Cook on for 20 minutes, turning 10 minutes in.
5. Check the temperature before serving. Chicken should be at least 74°C/165°F internally before serving.

Air Fryer Chicken Wings With Honey And Sesame

Servings: 1-2

Cooking Time: 10-30 Mints

Ingredients:

- 450–500g /2 oz chicken wings with tips removed
- 1 tbsp olive oil
- 3 tbsp cornflour
- 1 tbsp runny honey
- 1 tsp soy sauceor tamari
- 1 tsp rice wine vinegar
- 1 tsp toasted sesame oil
- 2 tsp sesame seeds, toasted
- 1 large spring onion, thinly sliced
- salt and freshly ground black pepper

Directions:

1. In a large bowl, toss together the chicken wings, olive oil and a generous amount of salt and pepper. Toss in the cornflour, a tablespoon at a time, until the wings are well coated.

2. Air-fry the chicken wings in a single layer for 25 minutes at 180°C/350°F, turning halfway through the cooking time.

3. Meanwhile, make the glaze by whisking together the honey, soy sauce, rice wine vinegar and toasted sesame oil in a large bowl.

4. Tip the cooked wings into the glaze, tossing until they're well coated. Return to the air fryer in a single layer for 5 more minutes.

5. Toss the wings once more in any remaining glaze. Sprinkle with toasted sesame seeds and spring onion and serve.

Air Fryer Spicy Chiken Thights

Servings: 4

Cooking Time: 10 Mints

Ingredients:

- 80 ml low-sodium soy sauce
- 60 ml extra-virgin olive oil
- 2 tbsp. honey
- 2 tbsp. chilli garlic sauce
- Juice of 1 lime
- 2 cloves garlic, crushed
- 2 tsp. freshly grated ginger
- 4 bone-in, skin-on chicken thighs
- Thinly sliced spring onions, for garnish
- Toasted sesame seeds, for garnish

Directions:

1. In a large bowl, combine soy sauce, oil, honey, chilli garlic sauce, lime juice, garlic, and ginger. Reserve 120ml of marinade. Add chicken thighs to bowl and toss to coat. Cover and refrigerate for at least 30 minutes.

2. Remove 2 thighs from marinade and place in basket of air fryer. Cook at 200°C/400°F until thighs are cooked through to an internal temperature of 73°C/165°F, 15 to 20 minutes. Transfer thighs to a plate and tent with foil. Repeat with remaining thighs.

3. Meanwhile, in a small saucepan over medium heat, bring reserved marinade to a boil. Reduce heat and simmer until sauce thickens slightly, 4 to 5 minutes.

4. Brush sauce over thighs and garnish with spring onions and sesame seeds before serving

Air Fryer Frozen Chicken Cordon Bleu

Servings: 1
Cooking Time: 15 Mints
Ingredients:

- 1 frozen chicken cordon bleu

Directions:

1. Preheat air fryer to 180°C/350°F, for approximately 2-3 minutes.
2. Place frozen chicken cordon bleu in an air fryer basket. If you are cooking more than one, ensure they are not touching.
3. Air fry cordon bleu for: 15-20 minutes for frozen pre-cooked cordon bleu, or - 30-35 minutes for frozen raw cordon bleu See note 2.
4. When cooking time is up, check internal temperature to make sure cordon bleu have reached at least 74°C/165°F in the center of the thickest part. If required, air fry for additional 2-3 minute intervals until the correct temperature is reached

Air Fryer Fried Chicken

Servings: 3
Cooking Time: 10 Mints
Ingredients:

- 900 g bone-in skin-on chicken pieces (mix of cuts)
- 480 ml buttermilk
- 120 ml hot sauce
- 3 tsp. salt
- 250 g plain flour
- 1 tsp. garlic powder
- 1 tsp. onion powder
- 1/2 tsp. oregano
- 1/2 tsp. freshly ground black pepper
- 1/4 tsp. cayenne pepper

Directions:

1. Trim chicken of excess fat and place in a large bowl. In a medium bowl, combine buttermilk, hot sauce, and 2 teaspoons salt.
2. Pour mixture over chicken, making sure all pieces are coated. Cover and refrigerate for at least 1 hour and up to overnight.
3. In a shallow bowl or pie dish, combine flour, remaining 1 teaspoon salt, and seasonings. Working with one at a time, remove chicken from buttermilk, shaking off excess buttermilk. Place in flour mixture, turning to coat.
4. Place coated chicken in basket of air fryer, working in batches as necessary to not overcrowd the basket. Cook at 200°C/400°F until chicken is golden and internal temperature reaches 73°C/165°F, 20 to 25 minutes, flipping halfway through.
5. Repeat with remaining chicken

Beef & Lamb And Pork Recipes
Honey & Mustard Meatballs

Servings: 4

Ingredients:

- 500g minced pork
- 1 red onion
- 1 tsp mustard
- 2 tsp honey
- 1 tsp garlic puree
- 1 tsp pork seasoning
- Salt and pepper

Directions:

1. Thinly slice the onion
2. Place all the ingredients in a bowl and mix until well combined
3. Form into meatballs, place in the air fryer and cook at 180°C for 10 minutes

Air Fryer Pork Bratwurst

Servings: 2

Ingredients:

- 2 pork bratwursts
- 2 hotdog bread rolls
- 2 tbsp tomato sauce

Directions:

1. Preheat the air fryer to 200°C
2. Place the bratwurst in the fryer and cook for 10 minutes, turning halfway
3. Remove and place in the open bread rolls
4. Place back into the air fryer for 1 to 2 minutes, until the read is slightly crisped
5. Enjoy with the tomato sauce either on top or on the side

Breaded Pork Chops

Servings: 6

Ingredients:

- 6 boneless pork chops
- 1 beaten egg
- 100g panko crumbs
- 75g crushed cornflakes
- 2 tbsp parmesan
- 1 ¼ tsp paprika
- ½ tsp garlic powder
- ½ tsp onion powder
- ¼ tsp chilli powder
- Salt and pepper to taste

Directions:

1. Heat the air fryer to 200ºC
2. Season the pork chops with salt
3. Mix the panko, cornflakes, salt, parmesan, garlic powder, onion powder, paprika, chilli powder and pepper in a bowl
4. Beat the egg in another bowl
5. Dip the pork in the egg and then coat with panko mix
6. Place in the air fryer and cook for about 12 minutes turning halfway

Copycat Burger

Servings: 4

Ingredients:

- 400g minced pork
- 4 wholemeal burger buns
- Avocado sauce to taste
- 1 avocado
- 1 small onion, chopped
- 2 chopped spring onions
- Salad garnish
- 1 tbsp Worcester sauce
- 1 tbsp tomato ketchup
- 1 tsp garlic puree
- 1 tsp mixed herbs

Directions:

1. In a bowl mix together the mince, onion, half the avocado and all of the seasoning
2. Form into burgers
3. Place in the air fryer and cook at 180ºC for 8 minutes
4. When cooked place in the bun, layer with sauce and salad garnish

Beef Kebobs

Servings: 4

Ingredients:

- 500g cubed beef
- 25g low fat sour cream
- 2 tbsp soy sauce
- 8 x 6 inch skewers
- 1 bell pepper
- Half an onion

Directions:

1. Mix the sour cream and soy sauce in a bowl, add the cubed beef and marinate for at least 30 minutes
2. Cut the pepper and onion into 1 inch pieces, soak the skewers in water for 10 minutes
3. Thread beef, bell peppers and onion onto skewers
4. Cook in the air fryer at 200ºC for 10 minutes turning halfway

Cheesy Meatball Sub

Servings: 2

Ingredients:

- 8 frozen pork meatballs
- 5 tbsp marinara sauce
- 160g grated parmesan cheese
- 2 sub rolls or hotdog rolls
- 1/4 tsp dried oregano

Directions:

1. Preheat the air fryer to 220ºC
2. Place the meatball in the air fryer and cook for around 10 minutes, turning halfway through
3. Place the marinara sauce in a bowl
4. Add the meatballs to the sauce and coat completely
5. Add the oregano on top and coat once more
6. Take the bread roll and add the mixture inside
7. Top with the cheese
8. Place the meatball sub back in the air fryer and cook for 2 minutes until the bad is toasted and the cheese has melted

Air Fryer Bacon-wrapped Asparagus

Servings: 4
Cooking Time: 10 Mints
Ingredients:

- 12 asparagus spears
- 12 slices bacon
- 1 tablespoon light olive oil

Directions:

1. Preheat air fryer to 200°C/400°F.
2. Trim any woody bits from the ends of the asparagus spears, then wrap each asparagus spear with bacon, wrapping tightly from the bottom towards the top.
3. Lightly brush or spritz the air fryer basket with oil (optional, but recommended if your air fryer is prone to sticking). Then place the bacon wrapped asparagus in the air fryer in a single layer. Try to ensure it is not touching.
4. Air fry the asparagus for 10-15 minutes flipping it over halfway through the cooking time if required for your air fryer.
5. Cook until the bacon is crispy.

Meatloaf

Servings: 2
Ingredients:

- 500g minced pork
- 1 egg
- 3 tbsp breadcrumbs
- 2 mushrooms thickly sliced
- 1 tbsp olive oil
- 1 chopped onion
- 1 tbsp chopped thyme
- 1 tsp salt
- Ground black pepper

Directions:

1. Preheat air fryer to 200ºC
2. Combine all the ingredients in a bowl
3. Put the mix into a pan and press down firmly, coat with olive oil
4. Place pan in the air fryer and cook for 25 minutes

Asian Meatballs

Servings: 2

Ingredients:

- 500g minced pork
- 2 eggs
- 100g breadcrumbs
- 1 tsp minced garlic
- ⅓ tsp chilli flakes
- 1 tsp minced ginger
- 1 tsp sesame oil
- 1 tsp soy
- 2 diced spring onions
- Salt and pepper to taste

Directions:

1. Mix all ingredients in a bowl until combined
2. Form mix into 1 ½ inch meatballs
3. Place in the air fryer and cook at 200ºC for about 10 minutes until cooked

Lamb Burgers

Servings: 4

Ingredients:

- 600g minced lamb
- 2 tsp garlic puree
- 1 tsp harissa paste
- 2 tbsp Moroccan spice
- Salt and pepper

Directions:

1. Place all the ingredients in a bowl and mix well
2. Form into patties
3. Place in the air fryer and cook at 180ºC for 18 minutes

Jamaican Jerk Pork

Servings: 4

Ingredients:

- 400g pork butt cut into 3 pieces
- 100g jerk paste

Directions:

1. Rub the pork with jerk paste and marinate for 4 hours
2. Preheat air fryer to 190°C
3. Place pork in the air fryer and cook for about 20 minutes turning halfway

Air Fryer Pork Shoulder Steak

Servings: 3

Cooking Time: 15 Mints

Ingredients:

- 3 pork shoulder steaks.
- 1½ tsp Italian seasoning
- 1 tsp cumin
- 2 tsp garlic powder
- 1 tsp smoked paprika
- Salt and black pepper

Directions:

1. Preheat the air fryer to 400°F/200°C.

2. Put pork in a large bowl. Add Italian seasoning, cumin, garlic powder, smoked paprika, and salt and pepper. Massage pork steaks with seasonings until they are evenly coated on both sides.

3. Place the pork steaks in the air fryer in one layer and cook for 8 to 9 minutes. Then flip and cook for an additional 3-5 minutes. (The safe internal pork cooking temperature is 145°F/60°C.). Let rest for 3 minutes then serve.

4. Remove them from the air fryer and let sit for at least 3 minutes before cutting

Air Fryer Steak

Servings: 2

Cooking Time: 10 Mints

Ingredients:

- 57 g/4 tbsp. butter, softened
- 2 cloves garlic, crushed
- 2 tsp. freshly chopped parsley
- 1 tsp. freshly chopped chives
- 1 tsp. freshly chopped thyme
- 1 tsp. freshly chopped rosemary
- 900 g bone-in ribeye
- Salt
- Freshlyground black pepper

Directions:

1. In a small bowl, combine butter and herbs. Place in centre of a piece of cling film and roll into a log. Twist ends together to keep tight and refrigerate until hardened, 20 minutes.

2. Season steak on both sides with salt and pepper.

3. Place steak in basket of air fryer and cook at 200°C/400°F for 12 to 14 minutes, for medium, depending on thickness of steak, flipping halfway through.

4. Top steak with a slice of herb butter to serve

Air Fryer Pork Belly With Christmas Glaze

Servings: 4

Cooking Time: 55 Mints

Ingredients:

- 1 tbsp sea salt
- 1kg piece pork belly, rind dried
- 4-6 small pink lady apples
- Steamed green beans, to serve, optional
- Christmas glaze
- 125 ml/½ cup maple syrup
- 60 ml/¼ cup apple cider vinegar
- 55 g/¼ cup caster sugar
- 2 tsp wholegrain mustard
- ½ tsp mixed spice
- 40 g butter, chilled, chopped

Directions:

1. Preheat an air fyer to 200°C/400°F for 3 minutes. Rub salt into pork rind. Spray air fryer basket with oil. Place pork in prepared basket. Spray the pork with oil. Air fry for 25 minutes or until the pork crackles. Reduce temperature to 160°C/320°F. Add apples to the air fryer basket. Air fry for a further 30 minutes or until the pork is tender and cooked through.

2. Meanwhile, make the glaze. Place maple syrup , vinegar , sugar , mustard and mixed spice in a small saucepan over medium heat. Bring to a boil. Reduce heat and simmer for 5 minutes or until glaze is thick and syrupy. Stir through cold butter .

3. Slice pork and arrange on a serving plate. Serve with apples and steamed green beans, if using. Drizzle over the glaze to serve.

Japanese Pork Chops

Servings: 4

Ingredients:

- 6 boneless pork chops
- 30g flour
- 2 beaten eggs
- 2 tbsp sweet chilli sauce
- 500g cup seasoned breadcrumbs
- ⅛ tsp salt
- ⅛ tsp pepper
- Tonkatsu sauce to taste

Directions:

1. Place the flour, breadcrumbs and eggs in 3 separate bowls
2. Sprinkle both sides of the pork with salt and pepper
3. Coat the pork in flour, egg and then breadcrumbs
4. Place in the air fryer and cook at 180ºC for 8 minutes, turn then cook for a further 5 minutes
5. Serve with sauces on the side

Pork Chops With Sprouts

Servings: 2

Ingredients:

- 300g pork chops
- ⅛ tsp salt
- ½ tsp pepper
- 250g Brussels sprouts quartered
- 1 tsp olive oil
- 1 tsp maple syrup
- 1 tsp dijon mustard

Directions:

1. Season the pork chops with salt and pepper
2. Mix together oil, maple syrup and mustard. Add Brussels sprouts
3. Add pork chops and Brussels sprouts to the air fryer and cook at 200ºC for about 10 minutes

Honey & Mustard Sausages With Potatoes, Peppers & Onions

Servings: 2

Ingredients:

- 400 g/14 oz. baby new potatoes
- 1 onion, chopped into 4 wedges
- 1 tablespoon olive oil
- 1 tablespoon runny honey
- 1 tablespoon wholegrain mustard
- 6 sausages
- 5 baby (bell) peppers, roughly chopped
- salt and freshly ground black pepper
- fresh rosemary sprigs, to garnish

Directions:

1. Preheat the air-fryer to 180°C/350°F.
2. Chop any larger potatoes to 3 cm/1¼ in. in length (leave any smaller potatoes whole). Toss the potatoes and onion wedges in the oil with salt and pepper to taste. Add the potatoes and onion wedges to the preheated air-fryer and air-fry for 10 minutes.
3. Meanwhile, mix together the honey and mustard, then toss the sausages in the honey-mustard mixture until evenly covered. Add these to the air-fryer and cook for a further 6 minutes. Toss the food in the air-fryer and add the (bell) peppers, stir everything well and air-fry for a further 7 minutes. Tip on to a serving platter, garnish with fresh rosemary sprigs if you wish and serve.

Pork Belly With Crackling

Servings: 4

Ingredients:

- 800g belly pork
- 1 tsp sea salt
- 1 tsp garlic salt
- 2 tsp five spice
- 1 tsp rosemary
- 1 tsp white pepper
- 1 tsp sugar
- Half a lemon

Directions:

1. Cut lines into the meat portion of the belly pork
2. Cook thoroughly in water
3. Allow to air dry for 3 hours
4. Score the skin and prick holes with a fork
5. Rub with the dry rub mix, rub some lemon juice on the skin
6. Place in the air fryer and cook at 160°C for 30 minutes then at 180°C for a further 30 minutes

Steak Popcorn Bites

Servings: 4

Ingredients:

- 500g steak, cut into 1" sized cubes
- 500g potato chips, ridged ones work best
- 100g flour
- 2 beaten eggs
- Salt and pepper to taste

Directions:

1. Place the chips into the food processor and pulse unit you get fine chip crumbs
2. Take a bowl and combine the flour with salt and pepper
3. Add the chips to another bowl and the beaten egg to another bowl
4. Take the steak cubes and dip first in the flour, then the egg and then the chip crumbs
5. Preheat your air fryer to 260°C
6. Place the steak pieces into the fryer and cook for 9 minutes

Lamb Calzone

Servings: 2

Ingredients:

- 1 tsp olive oil
- 1 chopped onion
- 100g baby spinach leaves
- 400g minced pork
- 250g whole wheat pizza dough
- 300g grated cheese

Directions:

1. Heat the olive oil in a pan, add the onion and cook for about 2 minutes
2. Add the spinach and cook for a further 1 ½ minutes
3. Stir in marinara sauce and the minced pork
4. Divide the dough into four and roll out into circles
5. Add ¼ of filling to each piece of dough
6. Sprinkle with cheese and fold the dough over to create half moons, crimp edges to seal
7. Spray with cooking spray, place in the air fryer and cook at 160°C for 12 minutes turning after 8 minutes

Traditional Pork Chops

Servings: 8

Ingredients:

- 8 pork chops
- 1 egg
- 100ml milk
- 300g bread crumbs
- 1 packet of dry ranch seasoning mix
- Salt and pepper to taste

Directions:

1. Preheat air fryer to 170°C
2. Beat the egg in a bowl, add the milk season with salt and pepper
3. In another bowl mix the bread crumbs and ranch dressing mix
4. Dip the pork into the egg then cover with breadcrumbs
5. Place in the air fryer and cook for 12 minutes turning half way

Mustard Pork Tenderloin

Servings: 2

Ingredients:

- 1 pork tenderloin
- 3 tbsp soy sauce
- 2 minced garlic cloves
- 3 tbsp olive oil
- 2 tbsp brown sugar
- 1 tbsp dijon mustard
- Salt and pepper for seasoning

Directions:

1. Take a bowl and combine the ingredients, except for the pork
2. Pour the mixture into a ziplock bag and then add the pork
3. Close the top and make sure the pork is well covered
4. Place in the refrigerator for 30minutes
5. Preheat your air fryer to 260°C
6. Remove the pork from the bag and place in the fryer
7. Cook for 25 minutes, turning halfway
8. Remove and rest for 5 minutes before slicing into pieces

Fish & Seafood Recipes
Crispy Nacho Prawns

Servings: 6

Ingredients:

- 1 egg
- 18 large prawns
- 1 bag of nacho cheese flavoured corn chips, crushed

Directions:

1. Wash the prawns and pat dry
2. Place the chips into a bowl
3. In another bowl, whisk the egg
4. Dip the prawns into the egg and then the nachos
5. Preheat the air fryer to 180ºC
6. Cook for 8 minutes

Cajun Shrimp Boil

Servings: 6

Ingredients:

- 300g cooked shrimp
- 14 slices of smoked sausage
- 5 par boiled potatoes, cut into halves
- 4 mini corn on the cobs, quartered
- 1 diced onion
- 3 tbsp old bay seasoning
- Olive oil spray

Directions:

1. Combine all the ingredients in a bowl and mix well
2. Line the air fryer with foil
3. Place half the mix into the air fryer and cook at 200ºC for about 6 minutes, mix the ingredients and cook for a further 6 minutes.
4. Repeat for the second batch

Air Fryer Crab Cakes

Servings: 6
Cooking Time: 5 Mins

Ingredients:

- 60 g mayonnaise
- 1 egg
- 2 tbsp. chives, finely chopped
- 2 tsp. Dijon mustard
- 2 tsp. cajun seasoning
- 1 tsp. lemon zest
- 1/2 tsp. salt
- 450 g jumbo lump crab meat
- 120 g Cracker crumbs (from about 20 crackers)
- Cooking spray
- Hot sauce, for serving
- Lemon wedges, for serving
- FOR THE TARTAR SAUCE
- 60 g mayonnaise
- 80 1/2 g dill pickle, finely chopped
- 1 tbsp. shallot, finely chopped
- 2 tsp. capers, finely chopped
- 1 tsp. fresh lemon juice
- 1/4 tsp. Dijon mustard
- 1 tsp. fresh dill, finely chopped

Directions:

1. Make crab cakes: In a large bowl, whisk together mayo, egg, chives, Dijon mustard, cajun seasoning, lemon zest and salt. Fold in the crab meat and the cracker crumbs.

2. Divide the mixture equally, forming 8 patties. You can refrigerate them for up to 4 hours if you're not ready to fry them. (Patties can also be frozen on a parchment-lined baking tray.)

3. Heat the air fryer to 190°C/375°F and spray the basket and the tops of the crab cakes with cooking spray. Place the crab cakes into the basket in a single layer. Cook until deep golden brown and crisp, about 12-14 minutes, flipping halfway through.

4. Meanwhile, make tartar sauce: Combine all of the tartar sauce ingredients in a bowl.

5. Serve the crab cakes warm with hot sauce, lemon wedges, and tartar sauce.

Ranch Style Fish Fillets

Servings: 4

Ingredients:

- 200g bread crumbs
- 30g ranch-style dressing mix
- 2 tbsp oil
- 2 beaten eggs
- 4 fish fillets of your choice
- Lemon wedges to garnish

Directions:

1. Preheat air fryer to 180°C
2. Mix the bread crumbs and ranch dressing mix together, add in the oil until the mix becomes crumbly
3. Dip the fish into the, then cover in the breadcrumb mix
4. Place in the air fryer and cook for 12-13 minutes

Air Fryer Mussels

Servings: 2

Ingredients:

- 400g mussels
- 1 tbsp butter
- 200ml water
- 1 tsp basil
- 2 tsp minced garlic
- 1 tsp chives
- 1 tsp parsley

Directions:

1. Preheat air fryer to 200°C
2. Clean the mussels, soak for 30 minutes, and remove the beard
3. Add all ingredients to an air fryer-safe pan
4. Cook for 3 minutes
5. Check to see if the mussels have opened, if not cook for a further 2 minutes. Once all mussels are open, they are ready to eat.

Cajun Prawn Skewers

Servings: 2

Ingredients:

- 350 g/12 oz. king prawns/jumbo shrimp
- MARINADE
- 1 teaspoon smoked paprika
- 1 teaspoon unrefined sugar
- 1 teaspoon salt
- ½ teaspoon onion powder
- ½ teaspoon mustard powder
- ¼ teaspoon dried oregano
- ¼ teaspoon dried thyme
- 1 teaspoon white wine vinegar
- 2 teaspoons olive oil

Directions:

1. Mix all the marinade ingredients together in a bowl. Mix the prawns/shrimp into the marinade and cover. Place in the fridge to marinate for at least an hour.
2. Preheat the air-fryer to 180°C/350°F.
3. Thread 4–5 prawns/shrimp on to each skewer (you should have enough for 4–5 skewers). Add the skewers to the preheated air-fryer and air-fry for 2 minutes, then turn the skewers and cook for a further 2 minutes. Check the internal temperature of the prawns/shrimp has reached at least 50°C/125°F using a meat thermometer – if not, cook for another few minutes. Serve immediately.

Air Fried Popcorn Shrimp With Mango And Avocado Salad

Servings: 4

Cooking Time: 10 Mints

Ingredients:

- 1/2 lemon, juice and finely grated zest
- 2 tablespoons extra virgin olive oil
- 1 teaspoon honey
- 1/4 teaspoon salt fresh ground pepper to taste
- For the salad:
- 1 package Gorton's Popcorn Shrimp
- 100 g/4 cups mixed greens
- 1 mango, diced
- 1 avocado, diced
- 1 small cucumber, sliced

Directions:

1. Cook the half of the bag of the Popcorn Shrimp in your air fryer at 200°C/400°F for 8 – 10 minutes, until reaching an internal temperature of 165°C/320°F or higher.
2. In a small bowl, add the dressing ingredients and mix well.
3. In a large bowl, combine the greens, mango, avocado and cucumber.
4. Top with the shrimp when ready and drizzle with the dressing. Enjoy!

Copycat Fish Fingers

Servings: 2

Ingredients:

- 2 slices wholemeal bread, grated into breadcrumbs
- 50g plain flour
- 1 beaten egg
- 1 white fish fillet
- The juice of 1 small lemon
- 1 tsp parsley
- 1 tsp thyme
- 1 tsp mixed herbs
- Salt and pepper to taste

Directions:

1. Preheat the air fryer to 180ºC
2. Add salt pepper and parsley to the breadcrumbs and combine well
3. Place the egg in another bowl
4. Place the flour in a separate bowl
5. Place the fish into a food processor and add the lemon juice, salt, pepper thyme and mixed herbs
6. Blitz to create a crumb-like consistency
7. Roll your fish in the flour, then the egg and then the breadcrumbs
8. Cook at 180ºC for 8 minutes

Air Fryer Coconut Prawns

Servings: 4

Cooking Time: 5 Mins

Ingredients:

- 65 g plain flour
- Salt
- Freshlyground black pepper
- 100 g panko bread crumbs
- 35 g shredded sweetened coconut
- 2 large eggs, beaten
- 450 g large prawns, peeled and deveined, tails on
- FOR THE DIPPING SAUCE
- 120 gmayonnaise
- 1 tbsp. Sriracha
- 1 tbsp. Thai sweet chilli sauce

Directions:

1. In a shallow bowl, season flour with salt and pepper. In another shallow bowl, combine bread crumbs and coconut. Place eggs in a third shallow bowl.
2. Working with one at a time, dip prawns in flour, then eggs, then coconut mixture.
3. Place prawns in the basket of an air fryer and heat to 200°C/400°F. Bake until prawns are golden and cooked through, 10 to 12 minutes. Work in batches as necessary.
4. In a small bowl, combine mayonnaise, Sriracha, and chilli sauce. Serve prawns with dipping sauce

Cod In Parma Ham

Servings: 2

Ingredients:

- 2 x 175–190-g/6–7-oz. cod fillets, skin removed
- 6 slices Parma ham or prosciutto
- 16 cherry tomatoes
- 60 g/2 oz. rocket/arugula
- DRESSING
- 1 tablespoon olive oil
- 1½ teaspoons balsamic vinegar
- garlic salt, to taste
- freshly ground black pepper, to taste

Directions:

1. Preheat the air-fryer to 180ºC/350ºF.
2. Wrap each piece of cod snugly in 3 ham slices. Add the ham-wrapped cod fillets and the tomatoes to the preheated air-fryer and air-fry for 6 minutes, turning the cod halfway through cooking. Check the internal temperature of the fish has reached at least 60ºC/140ºF using a meat thermometer – if not, cook for another minute.
3. Meanwhile, make the dressing by combining all the ingredients in a jar and shaking well.
4. Serve the cod and tomatoes on a bed of rocket/arugula with the dressing poured over.

Air Fried Shrimp Manchurian

Servings: 4

Cooking Time: 20 Mints

Ingredients:

- 400 g Popcorn shrimp
- 3 garlic pods (minced)
- ½ inch ginger (grated)
- ½ of a medium-sized onion (cubed)
- 1 tbsp soya sauce 1 tsp chili garlic sauce
- 1 tbsp green chili sauce
- 1 tbsp tomato ketchup
- ½ tsp black pepper
- Corn flour slurry: 1 tbsp corn flour + 2 tbsp water (mixed)
- 2 spring onions (chopped)
- Oil (as required)

Directions:

1. Cook the half of the bag of the Popcorn Shrimp in your air fryer at 200°C/400°F for 8 – 10 minutes, until reaching an internal temperature of 165°C/320°F or higher.
2. Prepare the sauce by whisking soya sauce, chili garlic sauce, green chili sauce, tomato ketchup and black pepper in a bowl.
3. Heat oil in a pan, sauté ginger and garlic. Add the onions and sauté for 2 mins. Follow by adding the prepared sauce, corn flour slurry, and mix everything together.
4. Add the air fried Popcorn Shrimp, toss everything together to combine. Garnish with spring onions.
5. Serve hot! This dish goes well as a side with fried rice, white rice, or with hakka noodles, or is good as an appetizer on its own.

Beer Battered Fish Tacos

Servings: 2

Ingredients:

- 300g cod fillets
- 2 eggs
- 1 can of Mexican beer
- 300g cornstarch
- 300g flour
- 2 soft corn tortillas
- ½ tsp chilli powder
- 1 tbsp cumin
- Salt and pepper to taste

Directions:

1. Whisk together the eggs and beer
2. In a separate bowl whisk together cornstarch, chilli powder, flour, cumin and salt and pepper
3. Coat the fish in the egg mixture then coat in flour mixture
4. Spray the air fryer with non stick spray and add the fish
5. Set your fryer to 170ºC and cook for 15 minutes
6. Place the fish in a corn tortilla

Air Fryer Salmon

Servings: 2

Cooking Time: 5 Mins

Ingredients:

- 170 g salmon fillets
- Salt
- Freshly ground black pepper
- 2 tsp. extra-virgin olive oil
- 2 tbsp. whole grain mustard
- 1 tbsp. packed brown sugar
- 1 clove garlic, crushed
- 1/2 tsp. thyme leaves

Directions:

1. Season salmon all over with salt and pepper. In a small bowl, whisk together oil, mustard, sugar, garlic, and thyme. Spread on top of salmon.
2. Arrange salmon in an air fryer basket. Set air fryer to 200°C/400°F and cook for 10 minutes.

Oat & Parmesan Crusted Fish Fillets

Servings: 2

Ingredients:

- 20 g/⅓ cup fresh breadcrumbs
- 25 g/3 tablespoons oats
- 15 g/¼ cup grated Parmesan
- 1 egg
- 2 x 175-g/6-oz. white fish fillets, skin-on
- salt and freshly ground black pepper

Directions:

1. Preheat the air-fryer to 180°C/350°F.
2. Combine the breadcrumbs, oats and cheese in a bowl and stir in a pinch of salt and pepper. In another bowl beat the egg. Dip the fish fillets in the egg, then top with the oat mixture.
3. Add the fish fillets to the preheated air-fryer on an air-fryer liner or a piece of pierced parchment paper. Air-fry for 10 minutes. Check the fish is just flaking away when a fork is inserted, then serve immediately.

Air Fryer Orange Shrimp & Broccol

Servings: 3-4

Cooking Time: 20 Mints

Ingredients:

- 1 box Popcorn Shrimp
- 1 large or 2 small heads broccoli
- 1 tbsp olive oil
- 1/2 tsp salt
- 1/4 tsp pepper
- 85 ml orange juice
- 2 tbsp honey
- 2 tbsp soy sauce or coconut aminos
- 1 tsp minced garlic
- 1 tsp minced ginger
- 1 tsp sriracha or chili garlic sauce
- 1 tbsp cornstarch or arrowroot powder

Directions:

1. Toss broccoli crowns with olive oil, salt and pepper. Add to air fryer basket and air fry for 6 minutes at 200°C/400°F.
2. Remove broccoli from air fryer.
3. Cook the half of the bag of the Popcorn Shrimp in your air fryer at 200°C/400°F for 8 – 10 minutes, until reaching an internal temperature of 165°C/320°F or higher.
4. Make sauce by whisking together orange juice, honey, soy sauce, garlic, ginger, sriracha and cornstarch. Heat over low heat for 10-15 minutes, whisking occasionally until sauce thickens and becomes sticky.
5. Toss shrimp in about half the sauce to start. Add broccoli and toss to combine.
6. Serve with rice and the remaining sauce to dip or drizzle on top. Enjoy

Tandoori Salmon

Servings: 4

Ingredients:

- 300g salmon
- 1 tbsp butter
- 1 tbsp tandoori spice
- Salt and pepper to taste
- 1 small tomato
- Half a red onion
- 600g plain yogurt
- 30 fresh mint leaves, chopped
- 1 tsp minced green chilli
- 1 tbsp ground cumin
- Half a cucumber, chopped

Directions:

1. Cut the salmon into cubes and coat in the tandoori spice mix. Chill for 30 minutes to marinate
2. Blend mint, cumin and chilli with ¼ of the yogurt refrigerate and leave to steep
3. Peel the tomato and cut into cubes. Peel the cucumber and chop into cubes, finely dice the onion
4. Cook the salmon in the air fryer for 5-6 minutes at 200ºC
5. Mix the flavoured yogurt with the remaining yogurt, tomato, cucumber and onion
6. Place the sauce in serving bowls and place the salmon on top

Thai Salmon Patties

Servings: 7

Ingredients:

- 1 large can of salmon, drained and bones removed
- 30g panko breadcrumbs
- ¼ tsp salt
- 1 ½ tbsp Thai red curry paste
- 1 ½ tbsp brown sugar
- Zest of 1 lime
- 2 eggs
- Cooking spray

Directions:

1. Take a large bowl and combine all ingredients together until smooth
2. Use your hands to create patties that are around 1 inch in thickness
3. Preheat your air fryer to 180ºC
4. Coat the patties with cooking spray
5. Cook for 4 minutes each side

Mahi Fish Tacos

Servings: 4

Ingredients:

- 400g fresh mahi
- 8 small corn tortillas
- 2 tsp cajun seasoning
- 5 tbsp sour cream
- 2 tbsp mayonnaise
- 2 tbsp scotch bonnet pepper sauce (use 1 tbsp if you don't like your food too spicy)
- 1 tbsp sriracha sauce
- 2 tbsp lime juice
- Salt and pepper to taste
- 1 tbsp vegetable oil

Directions:

1. Clean the mahi. Cut into half inch slices and season with salt
2. Mix quarter parts cayenne pepper and black pepper with cajun seasoning. Sprinkle onto fish
3. Brush pepper sauce on both sides of the fish
4. Set the air fryer to 180ºC and cook for about 10 minutes or until golden brown
5. Whilst the fish cooks make the chipotle lime cream. Mix the mayo, sour cream, lime juice sriracha and cayenne pepper
6. Assemble tacos and enjoy

Air Fryer Tuna

Servings: 2

Ingredients:

- 2 tuna steaks, boneless and skinless
- 2 tsp honey
- 1 tsp grated ginger
- 4 tbsp soy sauce
- 1 tsp sesame oil
- 1/2 tsp rice vinegar

Directions:

1. Combine the honey, soy sauce, rice vinegar and sesame oil in a bowl until totally mixed together
2. Cover the tuna steaks with the sauce and place in the refrigerator for half an hour to marinade
3. Preheat the air fryer to 270ºC
4. Cook the tuna for 4 minutes
5. Allow to rest before slicing

Air Fried Fish Tostadas With Mango Salsa

Servings: 4
Cooking Time: 10 Mints

Ingredients:

- 4 tostada shells
- 8 Gorton's Beer Battered Fish Tenders
- 160 g fresh mango, diced
- 1 small jalapeno (about 2 Tablespoons), diced
- 1 Tablespoon fresh cilantro, minced
- 1 lime, juiced
- 1-2 Tablespoons red onion, minced salt to taste

Directions:

1. Cook your Gorton's Beer Battered Fish Tenders in the air fryer at 200°C/400°F for 9 – 10 minutes, until reaching an internal temperature of 165°C/320°F or higher.

2. While the Gorton's Seafood Beer Battered Fish Tenders are in the air fryer, prepare your mango salsa. Add mango, jalapeno, cilantro, lime, and red onion to a small bowl and mix until combined.

3. Place two Gorton's Seafood Beer Battered Fish Tenders on a single tostada shell then top with a healthy scoop of your fresh mango salsa. Enjoy!

Fish In Parchment Paper

Servings: 2

Ingredients:

- 250g cod fillets
- 1 chopped carrot
- 1 chopped fennel
- 1 tbsp oil
- 1 thinly sliced red pepper
- ½ tsp tarragon
- 1 tbsp lemon juice
- 1 tbsp salt
- ½ tsp ground pepper

Directions:

1. In a bowl, mix the tarragon and ½ tsp salt add the vegetables and mix well
2. Cut two large squares of parchment paper
3. Spray the cod with oil and cover both sides with salt and pepper
4. Place the cod in the parchment paper and add the vegetables
5. Fold over the paper to hold the fish and vegetables
6. Place in the air fryer and cook at 170ºC for 15 minutes

Air Fryer Fish Fillets

Servings: 3

Cooking Time: 15 Mints

Ingredients:

- 1 pound (454 g) white fish fillets (cod, halibut, tilapia, etc.)
- 1 teaspoon (5 ml) kosher salt , or to taste
- 1/2 teaspoon (2.5 ml) black pepper , or to taste
- 1 teaspoon (5 ml) garlic powder
- 1 teaspoon (5 ml) paprika
- 1-2 cups (60-120 g) breading of choice breadcrumbs, panko, crushed pork rinds or almond flour
- 1 egg , or more if needed

Directions:

1. Preheat the Air Fryer at 380°F/193°C for 4 minutes.
2. Cut fish filets in half if needed. Make sure they are even sized so they'll cook evenly.
3. Pat the filets dry. Lightly oil the filets and then season with salt, black pepper, garlic powder, and paprika.
4. Put the breading in a shallow bowl. In another bowl, beat the eggs. Dip the filets in the egg, shaking off excess egg. Dredge the filets in your breading of choice. Press filets into the bowl of breading so that they completely coat the filets. Repeat this process for all fish pieces.
5. Lightly spray parchment paper with oil spray. Lay coated fish in a single layer on parchment (cook in batches if needed). Generously spray all sides of the breaded filets with oil spray to coat any dry spots.
6. Air Fry at 380°F/193°C for 8-14 minutes, depending on the size and thickness of your filets. After 6 minutes, flip the filets. Lightly spray any dry spots than then continue cooking for the remaining time or until they are crispy brown and the fish is cooked through. Serve with your favorite dip: tartar sauce, mustard, aioli, etc

Side Dishes Recipes

Roasted Okra

Servings: 1

Ingredients:

- 300g Okra, ends trimmed and pods sliced
- 1 tsp olive oil
- ¼ tsp salt
- ⅛ tsp pepper

Directions:

1. Preheat the air fryer to 175ºC
2. Combine all ingredients in a bowl and stir gently
3. Place in the air fryer and cook for 5 minutes, shake and cook for another 5 minutes

Tex Mex Hash Browns

Servings: 4

Ingredients:

- 500g potatoes cut into cubes
- 1 tbsp olive oil
- 1 red pepper
- 1 onion
- 1 jalapeño pepper
- ½ tsp taco seasoning
- ½ tsp cumin
- Salt and pepper to taste

Directions:

1. Soak the potatoes in water for 20 minutes
2. Heat the air fryer to 160°C
3. Drain the potatoes and coat with olive oil
4. Add to the air fryer and cook for 18 minutes
5. Mix the remaining ingredients in a bowl, add the potatoes and mix well
6. Place the mix into the air fryer cook for 6 minutes, shake and cook for a further 5 minutes

Potato Hay

Servings: 4

Ingredients:

- 2 potatoes
- 1 tbsp oil
- Salt and pepper to taste

Directions:

1. Cut the potatoes into spirals
2. Soak in a bowl of water for 20 minutes, drain and pat dry
3. Add oil, salt and pepper and mix well to coat
4. Preheat air fryer to 180°C
5. Add potatoes to air fryer and cook for 5 minutes, toss then cook for another 12 until golden brown

Asparagus Fries

Servings: 2

Ingredients:

- 1 egg
- 1 tsp honey
- 100g panko bread crumbs
- Pinch of cayenne pepper
- 100g grated parmesan
- 12 asparagus spears
- 75g mustard
- 75g Greek yogurt

Directions:

1. Preheat air fryer to 200°C
2. Combine egg and honey in a bowl, mix panko crumbs and parmesan on a plate
3. Coat each asparagus in egg then in the bread crumbs
4. Place in the air fryer and cook for about 6 mins
5. Mix the remaining ingredients in a bowl and serve as a dipping sauce

Orange Tofu

Servings: 4

Ingredients:

- 400g tofu, drained
- 1 tbsp tamari
- 1 tbsp corn starch
- ¼ tsp pepper flakes
- 1 tsp minced ginger
- 1 tsp fresh garlic
- 1 tsp orange zest
- 75ml orange juice
- 75ml water
- 2 tsp cornstarch
- 1 tbsp maple syrup

Directions:

1. Cut the tofu into cubes, place in a bowl add the tamari and mix well
2. Mix in 1 tbsp starch and allow to marinate for 30 minutes
3. Place the remaining ingredients into another bowl and mix well
4. Place the tofu in the air fryer and cook at 190°C for about 10 minutes
5. Add tofu to a pan with sauce mix and cook until sauce thickens

Orange Sesame Cauliflower

Servings: 4

Ingredients:

- 100ml water
- 30g cornstarch
- 50g flour
- 1/2 tsp salt
- ½ tsp pepper
- 2 tbsp tomato ketchup
- 2 tbsp brown sugar
- 1 sliced onion

Directions:

1. Mix together flour, cornstarch, water, salt and pepper until smooth
2. Coat the cauliflower and chill for 30 minutes
3. Place in the air fryer and cook for 22 minutes at 170ºC
4. Meanwhile combine remaining ingredients in a saucepan, gently simmer until thickened.
5. Mix cauliflower with sauce and top with toasted sesame seeds to serve

Celery Root Fries

Servings: 2

Ingredients:

- ½ celeriac, cut into sticks
- 500ml water
- 1 tbsp lime juice
- 1 tbsp olive oil
- 75g mayo
- 1 tbsp mustard
- 1 tbsp powdered horseradish

Directions:

1. Put celeriac in a bowl, add water and lime juice, soak for 30 minutes
2. Preheat air fryer to 200
3. Mix together the mayo, horseradish powder and mustard, refrigerate
4. Drain the celeriac, drizzle with oil and season with salt and pepper
5. Place in the air fryer and cook for about 10 minutes turning halfway
6. Serve with the mayo mix as a dip

Homemade Croquettes

Servings:4
Cooking Time:15 Minutes

Ingredients:

- 400 g / 14 oz white rice, uncooked
- 1 onion, sliced
- 2 cloves garlic, finely sliced
- 2 eggs, beaten
- 50 g / 3.5 oz parmesan cheese, grated
- 1 tsp salt
- 1 tsp black pepper
- 50 g / 3.5 oz breadcrumbs
- 1 tsp dried oregano

Directions:

1. In a large mixing bowl, combine the white rice, onion slices, garlic cloves slices, one beaten egg, parmesan cheese, and a sprinkle of salt and pepper.
2. Whisk the second egg in a separate bowl and place the breadcrumbs into another bowl.
3. Shape the mixture into 12 even croquettes and roll evenly in the egg, followed by the breadcrumbs.
4. Preheat the air fryer to 190 °C / 375 °F and line the bottom of the basket with parchment paper.
5. Place the croquettes in the lined air fryer basket and cook for 15 minutes, turning halfway through, until crispy and golden. Enjoy while hot as a side to your main dish.

Garlic And Parsley Potatoes

Servings: 4

Ingredients:

- 500g baby potatoes, cut into quarters
- 1 tbsp oil
- 1 tsp salt
- ½ tsp garlic powder
- ½ tsp dried parsley

Directions:

1. Preheat air fryer to 175ºC
2. Combine potatoes and oil in a bowl
3. Add remaining ingredients and mix
4. Add to the air fryer and cook for about 25 minutes until golden brown, turning halfway through

Air Fryer Eggy Bread

Servings:2
Cooking Time:5-7 Minutes
Ingredients:
- 4 slices white bread
- 4 eggs, beaten
- 1 tsp black pepper
- 1 tsp dried chives

Directions:
1. Preheat your air fryer to 150 °C / 300 °F and line the bottom of the basket with parchment paper.
2. Whisk the eggs in a large mixing bowl and soak each slice of bread until fully coated.
3. Transfer the eggy bread to the preheated air fryer and cook for 5-7 minutes until the eggs are set and the bread is crispy.
4. Serve hot with a sprinkle of black pepper and chives on top.

Bbq Beetroot Crisps

Servings:4
Cooking Time:5 Minutes
Ingredients:
- 400 g / 14 oz beetroot, sliced
- 2 tbsp olive oil
- 1 tbsp BBQ seasoning
- ½ tsp black pepper

Directions:
1. Preheat the air fryer to 180 °C / 350 °F and line the bottom of the basket with parchment paper.
2. Place the beetroot slices in a large bowl. Add the olive oil, BBQ seasoning, and black pepper, and toss to coat the beetroot slices on both sides.
3. Place the beetroot slices in the air fryer and cook for 5 minutes until hot and crispy.

Cheesy Broccoli

Servings:4
Cooking Time:5 Minutes
Ingredients:

- 1 large broccoli head, broken into florets
- 4 tbsp soft cheese
- 1 tsp black pepper
- 50 g / 3.5 oz cheddar cheese, grated

Directions:

1. Preheat the air fryer to 150 °C / 300 °F and line the mesh basket with parchment paper or grease it with olive oil.
2. Wash and drain the broccoli florets and place in a bowl and stir in the soft cheese and black pepper to fully coat all of the florets.
3. Transfer the broccoli to the air fryer basket and sprinkle the cheddar cheese on top. Close the lid and cook for 5-7 minutes until the broccoli has softened and the cheese has melted.
4. Serve as a side dish to your favourite meal.

Ranch-style Potatoes

Servings: 2
Ingredients:

- 300g baby potatoes, washed
- 1 tbsp olive oil
- 3 tbsp dry ranch seasoning

Directions:

1. Preheat the air fryer to 220°C
2. Cut the potatoes in half
3. Take a mixing bowl and combine the olive oil with the ranch seasoning
4. Add the potatoes to the bowl and toss to coat
5. Cook for 15 minutes, shaking halfway through

Courgette Gratin

Servings: 2

Ingredients:

- 2 courgette
- 1 tbsp chopped parsley
- 2 tbsp breadcrumbs
- 4 tbsp grated parmesan
- 1 tbsp vegetable oil
- Salt and pepper to taste

Directions:

1. Heat the air fryer to 180°C
2. Cut each courgette in half length ways then slice
3. Mix the remaining ingredients together
4. Place the courgette in the air fryer and top with the breadcrumb mix
5. Cook for about 15 minutes until golden brown

Egg Fried Rice

Servings:2

Cooking Time:15 Minutes

Ingredients:

- 400 g / 14 oz cooked white or brown rice
- 100 g / 3.5 oz fresh peas and sweetcorn
- 2 tbsp olive oil
- 2 eggs, scrambled

Directions:

1. Preheat the air fryer to 150 °C / 300 °F and line the bottom of the basket with parchment paper.
2. In a bowl, mix the cooked white or brown rice and the fresh peas and sweetcorn.
3. Pour in 2 tbsp olive oil and toss to coat evenly. Stir in the scrambled eggs.
4. Transfer the egg rice into the lined air fryer basket, close the lid, and cook for 15 minutes until the eggs are cooked and the rice is soft.
5. Serve as a side dish with some cooked meat or tofu.

Sweet And Sticky Parsnips And Carrots

Servings:2
Cooking Time:15 Minutes

Ingredients:

- 4 large carrots, peeled and chopped into long chunks
- 4 large parsnips, peeled and chopped into long chunks
- 1 tbsp olive oil
- 2 tbsp honey
- 1 tsp dried mixed herbs

Directions:

1. Preheat the air fryer to 150 °C / 300 °F and line the bottom of the basket with parchment paper.
2. Place the chopped carrots and parsnips in a large bowl and drizzle over the olive oil and honey. Sprinkle in some black pepper to taste and toss well to fully coat the vegetables.
3. Transfer the coated vegetables into the air fryer basket and shut the lid. Cook for 20 minutes until the carrots and parsnips and cooked and crispy.
4. Serve as a side with your dinner.

Super Easy Fries

Servings: 2

Ingredients:

- 500g potatoes cut into ½ inch sticks
- 1 tsp olive oil
- ¼ tsp salt
- ¼ tsp pepper

Directions:

1. Place the potatoes in a bowl cover with water and allow to soak for 30 minutes
2. Spread the butter onto one side of the bread slices
3. Pat dry with paper, drizzle with oil and toss to coat
4. Place in the air fryer and cook at 200ºC for about 15 minutes, keep tossing through cooking time
5. Sprinkle with salt and pepper

Grilled Bacon And Cheese

Servings: 2

Ingredients:

- 4 slices of regular bread
- 1 tbsp butter
- 2 slices cheddar cheese
- 5 slices bacon, pre-cooked
- 2 slices mozzarella cheese

Directions:

1. Place the butter into the microwave to melt
2. Spread the butter onto one side of the bread slices
3. Place one slice of bread into the fryer basket, with the buttered side facing downwards
4. Place the cheddar on top, followed by the bacon, mozzarella and the other slice of bread, with the buttered side facing upwards
5. Set your fryer to 170ºC and cook the sandwich for 4 minutes
6. Turn the sandwich over and cook for another 3 minutes
7. Turn the sandwich out and serve whilst hot
8. Repeat with the other remaining sandwich

Zingy Roasted Carrots

Servings: 4

Ingredients:

- 500g carrots
- 1 tsp olive oil
- 1 tsp cayenne pepper
- Salt and pepper for seasoning

Directions:

1. Peel the carrots and cut them into chunks, around 2" in size
2. Preheat your air fryer to 220ºC
3. Add the carrots to a bowl with the olive oil and cayenne and toss to coat
4. Place in the fryer and cook for 15 minutes, giving them a stir halfway through
5. Season before serving

Cauliflower With Hot Sauce And Blue Cheese Sauce

Servings:2

Cooking Time:15 Minutes

Ingredients:

- For the cauliflower:
- 1 cauliflower, broken into florets
- 4 tbsp hot sauce
- 2 tbsp olive oil
- 1 tsp garlic powder
- ½ tsp salt
- ½ tsp black pepper
- 1 tbsp plain flour
- 1 tbsp corn starch
- For the blue cheese sauce:
- 50 g / 1.8 oz blue cheese, crumbled
- 2 tbsp sour cream
- 2 tbsp mayonnaise
- ½ tsp salt
- ½ tsp black pepper

Directions:

1. Preheat the air fryer to 180 °C / 350 °F and line the bottom of the basket with parchment paper.

2. In a bowl, combine the hot sauce, olive oil, garlic powder, salt, and black pepper until it forms a consistent mixture. Add the cauliflower to the bowl and coat in the sauce.

3. Stir in the plain flour and corn starch until well combined.

4. Transfer the cauliflower to the lined basket in the air fryer, close the lid, and cook for 12-15 minutes until the cauliflower has softened and is golden in colour.

5. Meanwhile, make the blue cheese sauce by combining all of the ingredients. When the cauliflower is ready, remove it from the air fryer and serve with the blue cheese sauce on the side.

Onion Rings

Servings: 4

Ingredients:

- 200g flour
- 75g cornstarch
- 2 tsp baking powder
- 1 tsp salt
- 2 pinches of paprika
- 1 large onion, cut into rings
- 1 egg
- 1 cup milk
- 200g breadcrumbs
- 2 pinches garlic powder

Directions:

1. Stir flour, salt, starch and baking powder together in a bowl
2. Dip onion rings into the flour mix to coat
3. Whisk the egg and milk into the flour mix, dip in the onion rings
4. Dip the onion rings into the bread crumbs
5. Heat the air fryer to 200ºC
6. Place the onion rings in the air fryer and cook for 2-3 minutes until golden brown
7. Sprinkle with paprika and garlic powder to serve

Pumpkin Fries

Servings: 4

Ingredients:

- 1 small pumpkin, seeds removed and peeled, cut into half inch slices
- 2 tsp olive oil
- 1 tsp garlic powder
- 1/2 tsp paprika
- A pinch of salt

Directions:

1. Take a large bowl and add the slices of pumpkin
2. Add the oil and all the seasonings. Toss to coat well
3. Place in the air fryer
4. Cook at 280ºC for 15 minutes, until the chips are tender, shaking at the halfway point

Vegetarian & Vegan Recipes
<u>Veggie Lasagne</u>

Servings: 1

Ingredients:

- 2 lasagne sheets
- Pinch of salt
- 100g pasta sauce
- 50g ricotta
- 60g chopped basil
- 40g chopped spinach
- 3 tbsp grated courgette

Directions:

1. Break the lasagne sheets in half, bring a pan of water to boil
2. Cook the lasagne sheets for about 8 minutes, drain and pat dry
3. Add 2 tbsp of pasta sauce to a mini loaf tin
4. Add a lasagne sheet, top with ricotta, basil and spinach, then add courgette
5. Place another lasagne sheet on top
6. Add a couple of tbsp pasta sauce, basil, spinach and courgette
7. Add the last lasagne sheet, top with pasta sauce and ricotta
8. Cover with foil and place in the air fryer
9. Cook at 180°C for 10 mins, remove foil and cook for another 3 minutes

Onion Dumplings

Servings: 2

Ingredients:

- 14 frozen dumplings (pierogies)
- 1 onion
- 1 tbsp olive oil
- 1 tsp sugar

Directions:

1. Take a large saucepan and fill with water, bringing to the boil
2. Cook the dumplings for 5 minutes, remove and drain
3. Slice the onion into long pieces
4. Oil the air fryer basket and preheat to 220°C
5. Cook the onion for 12 minutes, stirring often. After 5 minutes, add the sugar and combine
6. Remove the onions and place to one side
7. Add the dumplings to the air fryer and cook for 4 minutes
8. Turn the temperature up to 270°C and cook for another 3 minutes
9. Mix the dumplings with the onions before serving

Spanakopita Bites

Servings: 4

Ingredients:

- 300g baby spinach
- 2 tbsp water
- 100g cottage cheese
- 50g feta cheese
- 2 tbsp grated parmesan
- 1 tbsp olive oil
- 4 sheets of filo pastry
- 1 large egg white
- 1 tsp lemon zest
- 1 tsp oregano
- ¼ tsp salt
- ¼ tsp pepper
- ⅛ tsp cayenne

Directions:

1. Place spinach in water and cook for about 5 minutes, drain
2. Mix all ingredients together
3. Place a sheet of pastry down and brush with oil, place another on the top and do the same, continue until all four on top of each other
4. Ut the pastry into 8 strips then cut each strip in half across the middle
5. Add 1 tbsp of mix to each piece of pastry
6. Fold one corner over the mix to create a triangle, fold over the other corner to seal
7. Place in the air fryer and cook at 190ºC for about 12 minutes until golden brown

Aubergine Parmigiana

Servings: 2 As A Main Or 4 As A Side

Ingredients:

- 2 small or 1 large aubergine/eggplant, sliced 5 mm/¼ in. thick
- 1 tablespoon olive oil
- ¾ teaspoon salt
- 200 g/7 oz. mozzarella, sliced
- ½ teaspoon freshly ground black pepper
- 20 g/¼ cup finely grated Parmesan
- green vegetables, to serve
- SAUCE
- 135 g/5 oz. passata/strained tomatoes
- 1 teaspoon dried oregano
- ¼ teaspoon garlic salt
- 1 tablespoon olive oil

Directions:

1. Preheat the air-fryer to 200ºC/400ºF.

2. Rub each of the aubergine/eggplant slices with olive oil and salt. Divide the slices into two batches. Place one batch of the aubergine slices in the preheated air-fryer and air-fry for 4 minutes on one side, then turn over and air-fry for 2 minutes on the other side. Lay these on the base of a gratin dish that fits into your air-fryer.

3. Air-fry the second batch of aubergine slices in the same way. Whilst they're cooking, mix together the sauce ingredients in a small bowl.

4. Spread the sauce over the aubergines in the gratin dish. Add a layer of the mozzarella slices, then season with pepper. Add a second layer of aubergine slices, then top with Parmesan.

5. Place the gratin dish in the air-fryer and air-fry for 6 minutes, until the mozzarella is melted and the top of the dish is golden brown. Serve immediately with green vegetables on the side.

Vegan Fried Ravioli

Servings: 4

Ingredients:

- 100g panko breadcrumbs
- 2 tsp yeast
- 1 tsp basil
- 1 tsp oregano
- 1 tsp garlic powder
- Pinch salt and pepper
- 50ml liquid from can of chickpeas
- 150g vegan ravioli
- Cooking spray
- 50g marinara for dipping

Directions:

1. Combine the breadcrumbs, yeast, basil, oregano, garlic powder and salt and pepper
2. Put the liquid from the chickpeas in a bowl
3. Dip the ravioli in the liquid then dip into the breadcrumb mix
4. Heat the air fryer to 190ºC
5. Place the ravioli in the air fryer and cook for about 6 minutes until crispy

Buffalo Cauliflower Bites

Servings: 4

Ingredients:

- 3 tbsp ketchup
- 2 tbsp hot sauce
- 1 large egg white
- 200g panko bread crumbs
- 400g cauliflower
- ¼ tsp black pepper
- Cooking spray
- 40g sour cream
- 40g blue cheese
- 1 garlic clove, grated
- 1 tsp red wine vinegar

Directions:

1. Whisk together ketchup, hot sauce and egg white
2. Place the breadcrumbs in another bowl
3. Dip the cauliflower in the sauce then in the breadcrumbs
4. Coat with cooking spray
5. Place in the air fryer and cook at 160ºC for about 20 minutes until crispy
6. Mix remaining ingredients together and serve as a dip

Vegetarian Air Fryer Kimchi Bun

Servings: 4

Cooking Time: 20 Mints

Ingredients:

- 1300 g pack of Quorn Mince
- 1/2 cup chopped kimchi, save a splash of kimchi juice
- 2-3 chopped spring onions
- 1 egg
- 1 tbsp sesame oil
- 1 tbsp soy sauce
- 1 tsp white pepper powder
- Pinch of salt
- For the dough:
- 480 g flour
- 260 ml warm water
- 2 g salt

Directions:

1. Combine all the dough ingredients in a large bowl, mix well and shape into a ball. Let the dough rest for 10 minutes before kneading for 5 minutes and then resting for a further hour.

2. Mix all the remaining ingredients together, ensuring all liquid has been well absorbed by the Quorn Mince.

3. Lay out the dough on a lightly floured surface and cut into 16 equal pieces (about 30g/piece).

4. Wrap an equal amount of filling into each piece of dough, using your hands to form into a smooth and tightly wrapped bun.

5. Preheat air fryer to 180°C/350°F Place the buns into the air fryer and spray some oil over the top of each bun, cook for 10-15 mins until golden and enjoy!

Air Fryer Potatoes And Onions

Servings: 4

Cooking Time: 20 Mints

Ingredients:

- 908 g russet potatoes
- 2 medium red onions
- 3 tablespoons light olive oil
- 1 teaspoon fine sea salt

Directions:

1. Peel the potatoes, cut into 1-inch cubes, and place into a bowl of cold water to soak for at least 5 minutes.

2. Peel the onions, cut into quarters lengthwise, then cut each quarter in half through the middle.

3. Preheat air fryer to 180°C/350°F.

4. Drain the potatoes and pat them dry. Place the potato chunks and the onions into a large bowl, drizzle with oil, add the salt, and toss to coat.

5. Place the potatoes and onions in the air fryer basket and cook at 180°C/350°F for 20 minutes, shaking the basket to redistribute the potato cubes 1 or 2 times during the cooking time.

6. The potato cubes should be golden brown and the onions will be crispy. Air fry for additional 2-3 minute intervals if required.

Shakshuka

Servings: 2

Ingredients:

- 2 eggs
- BASE
- 100 g/3½ oz. thinly sliced (bell) peppers
- 1 red onion, halved and thinly sliced
- 2 medium tomatoes, chopped
- 2 teaspoons olive oil
- ¼ teaspoon salt
- ¼ teaspoon freshly ground black pepper
- ½ teaspoon chilli/hot red pepper flakes
- SAUCE
- 100 g/3½ oz. passata/strained tomatoes
- 1 tablespoon tomato purée/paste
- 1 teaspoon balsamic vinegar
- ½ teaspoon runny honey
- ½ teaspoon ground cumin
- ½ teaspoon paprika
- ¼ teaspoon salt
- ⅛ teaspoon freshly ground black pepper

Directions:

1. Preheat the air-fryer to 180ºC/350ºF.

2. Combine the base ingredients together in a baking dish that fits inside your air-fryer. Add the dish to the preheated air-fryer and air-fry for 10 minutes, stirring halfway through cooking.

3. Meanwhile, combine the sauce ingredients in a bowl. Pour this into the baking dish when the 10 minutes are up. Stir, then make a couple of wells in the sauce for the eggs. Crack the eggs into the wells, then cook for a further 5 minutes or until the eggs are just cooked and yolks still runny. Remove from the air-fryer and serve.

Air Fryer Tofu

Servings: 3-4
Cooking Time: 10 Mints
Ingredients:

- 1/2 tsp. onion powder
- 1/2 tsp. garlic powder
- 1/2 tsp. paprika (regular, hot or smoked)
- 395 g Firm tofu, cut into 3cm cubes
- 2 tbsp. low sodium soy sauce
- 2 tsp. toasted sesame oil
- 60 g cornflour
- 1 tsp. salt
- 1/4 tsp. Freshlyground black pepper
- Cooking spray
- 60 g mayonnaise
- 60 g Thai sweet chili sauce
- 2 tbsp. sriracha
- 2 cloves garlic, grated
- Steamed white rice, for serving
- Spring onions, sliced for garnish
- Sesame seeds, for garnish

Directions:

1. Toss tofu cubes, onion powder, garlic powder, paprika, soy sauce, and sesame oil in a large bowl. Toss well, cover, and transfer to the fridge to marinate for 20 minutes to an hour.

2. Preheat air fryer to 200ºC/400ºF. In a medium bowl, whisk together cornflour, salt and black pepper.

3. Working in batches if necessary, toss tofu in the cornstarch mixture until thoroughly coated. Shake off excess cornflour and add tofu in a single layer to the air fryer basket.

4. Spray the cubes with a bit of cooking spray and air fry the tofu for 15 minutes, tossing half way through, until it is golden and crispy.

5. Prepare the sauce: While the tofu cooks, in a large bowl, whisk together mayo, chilli sauce, sriracha, and grated garlic. Season to taste with salt and set aside.

6. When all the tofu is cooked, add the tofu and toss in the sauce. Serve over white rice, and garnish with spring onions and sesame seeds

Arancini

Servings: 12

Ingredients:

- 1 batch of risotto
- 100g panko breadcrumbs
- 1 tsp onion powder
- Salt and pepper
- 300ml warm marinara sauce

Directions:

1. Take ¼ cup risotto and form a rice ball
2. Mix the panko crumbs, onion powder, salt and pepper
3. Coat the risotto ball in the crumb mix
4. Place in the air fryer, spray with oil and cook at 200ºC for 10 minutes
5. Serve with marinara sauce

Ravioli Air Fryer Style

Servings: 4

Ingredients:

- Half a pack of frozen ravioli
- 200g Italian breadcrumbs
- 200ml buttermilk
- 5 tbsp marinara sauce
- 1 tbsp olive oil

Directions:

1. Preheat the air fryer to 220ºC
2. Place the buttermilk in a bowl
3. Add the breadcrumbs to another bowl
4. Take each piece of ravioli and dip it first into the buttermilk and then into the breadcrumbs, coating evenly
5. Add the ravioli to the air fryer and cook for 7 minutes, adding a small amount of oil at the halfway point
6. Serve with the marinara sauce on the side

Air Fryer Coconut Curried Cauliflower

Servings: 4

Cooking Time: 30 Mints

Ingredients:

- 3 tsp Keen's Traditional Curry Powder, plus ¼ tsp extra
- 1 tbsp garlic powder
- 2 tsp cooking salt
- 150 g /1 cup self-raising flour
- 270 ml can coconut cream
- 60 ml/¼ cup sparkling mineral water
- 1 egg
- ½ large cauliflower, cut into florets
- 200 g tub Greek-style yoghurt
- 2 tbsp mango chutney
- Fresh coriander leaves, to serve

Directions:

1. Whisk curry powder , garlic powder , salt and flour in a medium bowl. Whisk coconut cream, mineral water and egg in a separate medium bowl.

2. Working in batches, dip cauliflower florets in egg mixture, then coat in flour mixture, then re-coat in egg mixture and flour mixture, shaking off excess. Place in an air fryer, in a single layer.

3. Spray cauliflower florets with oil. Cook, in batches, at 200°C/400°F for 15 minutes, turning halfway through or until golden and tender.

4. Meanwhile, combine yoghurt , chutney and extra curry powder in a small serving bowl. Season.

5. Place cauliflower and yoghurt mixture on a serving plate. Sprinkle with coriander and ser

Tempura Veggies

Servings: 4

Ingredients:

- 150g flour
- ½ tsp salt
- ½ tsp pepper
- 2 eggs
- 2 tbsp cup water
- 100g avocado wedges
- 100g courgette slices
- 100g panko breadcrumbs
- 2 tsp oil
- 100g green beans
- 100g asparagus spears
- 100g red onion rings
- 100g pepper rings

Directions:

1. Mix together flour, salt and pepper. In another bowl mix eggs and water
2. Stir together panko crumbs and oil in a separate bowl
3. Dip vegetables in the flour mix, then egg and then the bread crumbs
4. Preheat the air fryer to 200°C
5. Place in the air fryer and cook for about 10 minutes until golden brown

Air Fryer Carrots Recipes

Servings: 2
Cooking Time: 15 Mints
Ingredients:

- 227 g carrots , peeled
- 2 teaspoons olive oil
- 1 teaspoon dried herbs (thyme, basil, mint, etc.)
- 1/2 teaspoon kosher salt , or to taste
- Black pepper, to taste

Directions:

1. Wash the fresh carrots. Slice the carrots diagonally in 1/2-inch thick slices. Combine the olive oil, herbs, salt & pepper in a bowl. Add the carrots and toss to evenly combine. Place the carrots in the air fryer basket.
2. Air Fry at 360°F/180°C for 10-15 minutes or until your desired texture.

Air-fried Artichoke Hearts

Servings: 7
Ingredients:

- 14 artichoke hearts
- 200g flour
- ¼ tsp baking powder
- Salt
- 6 tbsp water
- 6 tbsp breadcrumbs
- ¼ tsp basil
- ¼ tsp oregano
- ¼ tsp garlic powder
- ¼ tsp paprika

Directions:

1. Mix the baking powder, salt, flour and water in a bowl
2. In another bowl combine the breadcrumbs and seasonings
3. Dip the artichoke in the batter then coat in breadcrumbs
4. Place in the air fryer and cook at 180ºC for 8 minutes

Artichoke Crostini

Servings: 2

Ingredients:

- 100g cashews
- 1 tbsp olive oil
- 1 tbsp lemon juice
- 1 tsp balsamic vinegar
- 3 tbsp hummus
- 200g grilled artichoke hearts
- ½ tsp basil
- ½ tsp oregano
- ⅛ tsp onion powder
- 1 clove garlic minced
- Salt
- 1 baguette cut in ½ inch slices

Directions:

1. Combine cashews, olive oil, lemon juice, balsamic vinegar, basil oregano, onion powder, garlic and salt in a bowl. Set aside
2. Place the baguette slices in the air fryer and cook at 180ºC for 3-4 minutes
3. Sprinkle the baguette slices with cashew mix then add the artichoke hearts
4. Serve with hummus

Air Fryer Carrots Recipe

Servings: 2

Cooking Time: 20 Mints

Ingredients:

- 300 g baby carrots
- Spray oil
- Salt and pepper to taste

Directions:

1. Scrub your carrots clean.
2. Slice them lengthwise into 4 or 6 pieces.
3. Place your carrots in your air fryer basket.
4. Cook at 160°C/320°F for 10 minutes. Then turn up to 200°C/400°F for a further 10 minutes. Make sure to shake/turn the carrots when you turn the temperature up.

Crispy Sweet & Spicy Cauliflower

Servings: 2

Ingredients:

- ½ a head of cauliflower
- 1 teaspoon sriracha sauce
- 1 teaspoon soy sauce (or tamari)
- ½ teaspoon maple syrup
- 2 teaspoons olive oil or avocado oil

Directions:

1. Preheat the air-fryer to 180°C/350°F.
2. Chop the cauliflower into florets with a head size of roughly 5 cm/1 in. Place the other ingredients in a bowl and mix together, then add the florets and toss to coat them.
3. Add the cauliflower to the preheated air-fryer and air-fry for 12 minutes, shaking the drawer a couple of times during cooking.

Mediterranean Vegetables

Servings: 1–2

Ingredients:

- 1 courgette/zucchini, thickly sliced
- 1 (bell) pepper, deseeded and chopped into large chunks
- 1 red onion, sliced into wedges
- 12 cherry tomatoes
- 1 tablespoon olive oil
- ½ teaspoon salt
- ½ teaspoon freshly ground black pepper
- 2 rosemary twigs
- mozzarella, fresh pesto and basil leaves, to serve

Directions:

1. Preheat the air-fryer to 180°C/350°F.
2. Toss the prepared vegetables in the oil and seasoning. Add the vegetables and the rosemary to the preheated air-fryer and air-fry for 12–14 minutes, depending on how 'chargrilled' you like them.
3. Remove and serve topped with fresh mozzarella and pesto and scattered with basil leaves.

Flat Mushroom Pizzas

Servings: 1

Ingredients:

- 2 portobello mushrooms, cleaned and stalk removed
- 6 mozzarella balls
- 1 teaspoon olive oil
- PIZZA SAUCE
- 100 g/3½ oz. passata/strained tomatoes
- 1 teaspoon dried oregano
- ¼ teaspoon garlic salt

Directions:

1. Preheat the air-fryer to 180ºC/350ºF.

2. Mix the ingredients for the pizza sauce together in a small bowl. Fill each upturned portobello mushroom with sauce, then top each with three mozzarella balls and drizzle the olive oil over.

3. Add the mushrooms to the preheated air-fryer and air-fry for 8 minutes. Serve immediately.

Baked Aubergine Slices With Yogurt Dressing

Servings: 2

Ingredients:

- 1 aubergine/eggplant, sliced 1.5 cm/⅝ in. thick
- 3 tablespoons olive oil
- ½ teaspoon salt
- YOGURT DRESSING
- 1 small garlic clove
- 1 tablespoon tahini or nut butter
- 100 g/½ cup Greek yogurt
- 2 teaspoons freshly squeezed lemon juice
- 1 tablespoon runny honey
- a pinch of salt
- a pinch of ground cumin
- a pinch of sumac
- TO SERVE
- 30 g/1 oz. rocket/arugula
- 2 tablespoons freshly chopped mint
- 3 tablespoons pomegranate seeds

Directions:

1. Preheat the air-fryer to 180ºC/350ºF.

2. Drizzle the olive oil over each side of the aubergine/eggplant slices. Sprinkle with salt. Add the aubergines to the preheated air-fryer and air-fry for 10 minutes, turning halfway through cooking.

3. Meanwhile, make the dressing by combining all the ingredients in a mini food processor (alternatively, finely chop the garlic, add to a jar with the other ingredients and shake vigorously).

4. Serve the cooked aubergine slices on a bed of rocket/arugula, drizzled with the dressing and with the mint and pomegranate seeds scattered over the top.

Desserts Recipes
Mini Egg Buns

Servings: 8

Ingredients:

- 100g self raising flour
- 100g caster sugar
- 100g butter
- 2 eggs
- 2 tbsp honey
- 1 tbsp vanilla essence
- 300g soft cheese
- 100g icing sugar
- 2 packets of Mini Eggs

Directions:

1. Cream the butter and sugar together until light and fluffy, beat in the eggs one at a time
2. Add the honey and vanilla essence, fold in the flour a bit at a time
3. Divide the mix into 8 bun cases and place in the air fryer. Cook at 180°C for about 20 minutes
4. Cream the soft cheese and icing sugar together to make the topping
5. Allow the buns to cool, pipe on the topping mix and add mini eggs

Apple Chips With Yogurt Dip

Servings: 4

Ingredients:

- 1 apple
- 1 tsp cinnamon
- 2 tsp oil
- Cooking spray
- 25g greek yogurt
- 1 tbsp almond butter
- 1 tsp honey

Directions:

1. Thinly slice the apple, place in a bowl and coat with cinnamon and oil
2. Coat the air fryer with cooking spray and add the apple slices
3. Cook the slices for 12 minutes at 180°C
4. Mix the butter, honey and yogurt together and serve with the apple slices as a dip

Birthday Cheesecake

Servings: 8

Ingredients:

- 6 Digestive biscuits
- 50g melted butter
- 800g soft cheese
- 500g caster sugar
- 4 tbsp cocoa powder
- 6 eggs
- 2 tbsp honey
- 1 tbsp vanilla

Directions:

1. Flour a spring form tin to prevent sticking
2. Crush the biscuits and then mix with the melted butter, press into the bottom and sides of the tin
3. Mix the caster sugar and soft cheese with an electric mixer. Add 5 eggs, honey and vanilla. Mix well
4. Spoon half the mix into the pan and pat down well. Place in the air fryer and cook at 180ºC for 20 minutes then 160ºC for 15 minutes and then 150ºC for 20 minutes
5. Mix the cocoa and the last egg into the remaining mix. Spoon over the over the bottom layer and place in the fridge. Chill for 11 hours

Lava Cakes

Servings: 4

Ingredients:

- 1 ½ tbsp self raising flour
- 3 ½ tbsp sugar
- 150g butter
- 150g dark chocolate, chopped
- 2 eggs

Directions:

1. Preheat the air fryer to 175ºC
2. Grease 4 ramekin dishes
3. Melt chocolate and butter in the microwave for about 3 minutes
4. Whisk the eggs and sugar together until pale and frothy
5. Pour melted chocolate into the eggs and stir in the flour
6. Fill the ramekins ¾ full, place in the air fryer and cook for 10 minutes

Melting Moments

Servings: 9

Ingredients:

- 100g butter
- 75g caster sugar
- 150g self raising flour
- 1 egg
- 50g white chocolate
- 3 tbsp desiccated coconut
- 1 tsp vanilla essence

Directions:

1. Preheat the air fryer to 180ºC
2. Cream together the butter and sugar, beat in the egg and vanilla
3. Bash the white chocolate into small pieces
4. Add the flour and chocolate and mix well
5. Roll into 9 small balls and cover in coconut
6. Place in the air fryer and cook for 8 minutes and a further 6 minutes at 160ºC

Breakfast Muffins

Servings:4

Ingredients:

- 1 eating apple, cored and grated
- 40 g/2 heaped tablespoons maple syrup
- 40 ml/3 tablespoons oil (avocado, olive or coconut), plus extra for greasing
- 1 egg
- 40 ml/3 tablespoons milk (plant-based if you wish)
- 90 g/scant ¾ cup brown rice flour
- 50 g/½ cup ground almonds
- ¾ teaspoon ground cinnamon
- ⅛ teaspoon ground cloves
- ¼ teaspoon salt
- 1 teaspoon baking powder
- Greek or plant-based yogurt and fresh fruit, to serve

Directions:

1. In a bowl mix the grated apple, maple syrup, oil, egg and milk. In another bowl mix the rice flour, ground almonds, cinnamon, cloves, salt and baking powder. Combine the wet ingredients with the dry, mixing until there are no visible patches of the flour mixture left. Grease 4 ramekins and divide the batter equally between them.

2. Preheat the air-fryer to 160ºC/325ºF.

3. Add the ramekins to the preheated air-fryer and air-fry for 12 minutes. Check the muffins are cooked by inserting a cocktail stick/toothpick into the middle of one of the muffins. If it comes out clean, the muffins are ready; if not, cook for a further couple of minutes.

4. Allow to cool in the ramekins, then remove and serve with your choice of yogurt and fresh fruit.

Chocolate Souffle

Servings:2
Cooking Time:15 Minutes
Ingredients:

- 2 eggs
- 4 tbsp brown sugar
- 1 tsp vanilla extract
- 4 tbsp butter, melted
- 4 tbsp milk chocolate chips
- 4 tbsp flour

Directions:

1. Preheat the air fryer to 180 °C / 350 °F. Remove the mesh basket from the machine and line it with parchment paper.
2. Separate the egg whites from the egg yolks and place them in two separate bowls.
3. Beat the yolks together with the brown sugar, vanilla extract, melted butter, milk chocolate chips, and flour in a bowl. It should form a smooth, consistent mixture.
4. Whisk the egg whites until they form stiff peaks. In batches, fold the egg whites into the chocolate mixture.
5. Divide the batter evenly between two souffle dishes and place them in the lined air fryer basket.
6. Cook the souffle dishes for 15 minutes until hot and set.

Cherry Pies

Servings: 6
Ingredients:

- 300g prepared shortcrust pastry
- 75g cherry pie filling
- Cooking spray
- 3 tbsp icing sugar
- ½ tsp milk

Directions:

1. Cut out 6 pies with a cookie cutter
2. Add 1 ½ tbsp filling to each pie
3. Fold the dough in half and seal around the edges with a fork
4. Place in the air fryer, spray with cooking spray
5. Cook at 175°C for 10 minutes
6. Mix icing sugar and milk and drizzled over cooled pies to serve

Cinnamon-maple Pineapple Kebabs

Servings: 2

Ingredients:

- 4 x pineapple strips, roughly 2 x 2 cm/¾ x ¾ in. by length of pineapple
- 1 teaspoon maple syrup
- ½ teaspoon vanilla extract
- ¼ teaspoon ground cinnamon
- Greek or plant-based yogurt and grated lime zest, to serve

Directions:

1. Line the air-fryer with an air-fryer liner or a piece of pierced parchment paper. Preheat the air-fryer to 180ºC/350ºF.
2. Stick small metal skewers through the pineapple lengthways. Mix the maple syrup and vanilla extract together, then drizzle over the pineapple and sprinkle over the cinnamon.
3. Add the skewers to the preheated lined air-fryer and air-fry for 15 minutes, turning once. If there is any maple-vanilla mixture left after the initial drizzle, then drizzle this over the pineapple during cooking too. Serve with yogurt and lime zest.

Oat-covered Banana Fritters

Servings: 4

Ingredients:

- 3 tablespoons plain/all-purpose flour (gluten-free if you wish)
- 1 egg, beaten
- 90 g/3 oz. oatcakes (gluten-free if you wish) or oat-based cookies, crushed to a crumb consistency
- 1½ teaspoons ground cinnamon
- 1 tablespoon unrefined sugar
- 4 bananas, peeled

Directions:

1. Preheat the air-fryer to 180ºC/350ºF.
2. Set up three bowls – one with flour, one with beaten egg and the other with the oatcake crumb, cinnamon and sugar mixed together. Coat the bananas in flour, then in egg, then in the crumb mixture.
3. Add the bananas to the preheated air-fryer and air-fry for 10 minutes. Serve warm.

Lemon Tarts

Servings: 8

Ingredients:

- 100g butter
- 225g plain flour
- 30g caster sugar
- Zest and juice of 1 lemon
- 4 tsp lemon curd

Directions:

1. In a bowl mix together butter, flour and sugar until it forms crumbs, add the lemon zest and juice
2. Add a little water at a time and mix to form a dough
3. Roll out the dough and line 8 small ramekins with it
4. Add ¼ tsp of lemon curd to each ramekin
5. Cook in the air fryer for 15 minutes at 180°C

Thai Fried Bananas

Servings: 8

Ingredients:

- 4 ripe bananas
- 2 tbsp flour
- 2 tbsp rice flour
- 2 tbsp cornflour
- 2 tbsp desiccated coconut
- Pinch salt
- ½ tsp baking powder
- ½ tsp cardamon powder

Directions:

1. Place all the dry ingredients in a bowl and mix well. Add a little water at a time and combine to form a batter
2. Cut the bananas in half and then half again length wise
3. Line the air fryer with parchment paper and spray with cooking spray
4. Dip each banana piece in the batter mix and place in the air fryer
5. Cook at 200°C for 10 -15 minutes turning halfway
6. Serve with ice cream

Peanut Butter And Banana Bites

Servings: 12

Ingredients:

- 1 banana
- 12 wonton wrappers
- 75g peanut butter
- 1-2 tsp vegetable oil

Directions:

1. Slice the banana and place in a bowl of water with lemon juice to prevent browning
2. Place one piece of banana and a spoon of peanut butter in each wonton wrapper
3. Wet the edges of each wrapper and fold over to seal
4. Spray the air fryer with oil
5. Place in the air fryer and cook at 190°C for 6 minutes

Banana Maple Flapjack

Servings:9

Ingredients:

- 100 g/7 tablespoons butter (or plant-based spread if you wish)
- 75 g/5 tablespoons maple syrup
- 2 ripe bananas, mashed well with the back of a fork
- 1 teaspoon vanilla extract
- 240 g/2½ cups rolled oats/quick-cooking oats

Directions:

1. Gently heat the butter and maple syrup in a medium saucepan over a low heat until melted. Stir in the mashed banana, vanilla and oats and combine all ingredients. Pour the flapjack mixture into a 15 x 15-cm/6 x 6-in. baking pan and cover with foil.
2. Preheat the air-fryer to 200°C/400°F.
3. Add the baking pan to the preheated air-fryer and air-fry for 12 minutes, then remove the foil and cook for a further 4 minutes to brown the top. Leave to cool before cutting into 9 squares.

Peanut Butter & Chocolate Baked Oats

Servings:9

Ingredients:

- 150 g/1 heaped cup rolled oats/quick-cooking oats
- 50 g/⅓ cup dark chocolate chips or buttons
- 300 ml/1¼ cups milk or plant-based milk
- 50 g/3½ tablespoons Greek or plant-based yogurt
- 1 tablespoon runny honey or maple syrup
- ½ teaspoon ground cinnamon or ground ginger
- 65 g/scant ⅓ cup smooth peanut butter

Directions:

1. Stir all the ingredients together in a bowl, then transfer to a baking dish that fits your air-fryer drawer.
2. Preheat the air-fryer to 180ºC/350ºF.
3. Add the baking dish to the preheated air-fryer and air-fry for 10 minutes. Remove from the air-fryer and serve hot, cut into 9 squares.

Chocolate And Berry Pop Tarts

Servings:8

Cooking Time:10 Minutes

Ingredients:

- For the filling:
- 50 g / 1.8 oz fresh raspberries
- 50 g / 1.8 oz fresh strawberries
- 100 g / 3.5 oz granulated sugar
- 1 tsp corn starch
- For the pastry:
- 1 sheet puff pastry
- For the frosting:
- 4 tbsp powdered sugar
- 2 tbsp maple syrup or honey
- Chocolate sprinkles

Directions:

1. Preheat the air fryer to 180 °C / 350 °F and line the mesh basket with parchment paper or grease it with olive oil.
2. Make the filling by combining the strawberries, raspberries, and granulated sugar in a saucepan. Place on medium heat until the mixture starts to boil. When it begins to boil, turn the temperature down to a low setting. Use a spoon to break up the berries and forms a smooth mixture.
3. Stir in the corn starch and let the mixture simmer for 1-2 minutes. Remove the saucepan from the heat and set aside to cool while you prepare the pastry.
4. Roll out the large sheet of puff pastry and cut it into 8 equal rectangles.
5. Spoon 2 tbsp of the cooled berry filling onto one side of each rectangle. Fold over the other side of each puff pastry rectangle to cover the filling. Press the sides down with a fork or using your fingers to seal the filling into the pastry.
6. Transfer the puff pastry rectangles into the lined air fryer basket. Cook for 10-12 minutes until the pastry is golden and crispy.
7. Meanwhile, make the frosting. Whisk together the powdered sugar, maple syrup or honey, and chocolate chips in a bowl until well combined.
8. Carefully spread a thin layer of frosting in the centre of each pop tart. Allow the frosting to set before serving.

Chonut Holes

Servings: 12

Ingredients:

- 225g flour
- 75g sugar
- 1 tsp baking powder
- ¼ tsp cinnamon
- 2 tbsp sugar
- ½ tsp salt
- 2 tbsp aquafaba
- 1 tbsp melted coconut oil
- 75ml soy milk
- 2 tsp cinnamon

Directions:

1. In a bowl mix the flour, ¼ cup sugar, baking powder, ¼ tsp cinnamon and salt
2. Add the aquafaba, coconut oil and soy milk mix well
3. In another bowl mix 2 tsp cinnamon and 2 tbsp sugar
4. Line the air fryer with parchment paper
5. Divide the dough into 12 pieces and dredge with the cinnamon sugar mix
6. Place in the air fryer at 185°C and cook for 6-8 minutes, don't shake them

Blueberry Muffins

Servings: 12

Ingredients:

- 500g cups self raising flour
- 50g monk fruit
- 50g cream
- 225g oil
- 2 eggs
- 200g blueberries
- Zest and juice of 1 lemon
- 1 tbsp vanilla

Directions:

1. Mix together flour and sugar, set aside
2. In another bowl mix the remaining ingredients
3. Mix in the flour
4. Spoon the mix into silicone cupcake cases
5. Place in the air fryer and cook at 160°C for about 10 minutes

Chocolate Orange Fondant

Servings: 4

Ingredients:

- 2 tbsp self raising flour
- 4 tbsp caster sugar
- 115g dark chocolate
- 115g butter
- 1 medium orange rind and juice
- 2 eggs

Directions:

1. Preheat the air fryer to 180ºC and grease 4 ramekins
2. Place the chocolate and butter in a glass dish and melt over a pan of hot water, stir until the texture is creamy
3. Beat the eggs and sugar together until pale and fluffy
4. Add the orange and egg mix to the chocolate and mix
5. Stir in the flour until fully mixed together
6. Put the mix into the ramekins, place in the air fryer and cook for 12 minutes. Leave to stand for 2 minutes before serving

Thai Style Bananas

Servings: 4

Ingredients:

- 4 ripe bananas
- 2 tbsp flour
- 2 tbsp rice flour
- 2 tbsp corn flour
- 2 tbsp desiccated coconut
- Pinch salt
- ½ tsp baking powder
- Sesame seeds

Directions:

1. Add all the ingredients to a bowl apart from the sesame seeds mix well
2. Line the air fryer with foil
3. Dip the banana into the batter mix then roll in the sesame seeds
4. Place in the air fryer and cook for about 15 minutes at 200ºC turning halfway

Recipe Index

Printed in Great Britain
by Amazon

39009880R00059